Peter Arnott

Group Portrait in a Summer Landscape

Salamander Street

PLAYS

Wordville

INTRODUCTION

This play has been a very long time in the making. When these characters and their lovely house in Perthshire first started haunting me, the Berlin Wall was still standing – (just) – and my writing them down was an attempt at therapy as the past, present and future of the world I had grown up in were pulled from under my feet. And now, thirty years later, with the play still haunting me to the extent that I had to put a ghost in it, these characters have acquired a full theatrical life, animated and informed by a blisteringly strong cast and crew.

I can barely believe that it's happening. That it is happening in this place and time is down to a huge leap of faith in our post-pandemic theatrical universe-in-miniature here in Scotland that's been taken taken by Elizabeth Newman of Pitlochry Festival Theatre and David Grieg of the Lyceum in Edinburgh, the show's visionary director, and their coming together to put on a big new show that feels beautiful and sad and funny, that feels like it has a sense of history as well as a sense of humour.

I hope that their faith, and my thirty years of daydreaming, can come together in a memorable way where it really matters - in the audience. And that the swansong that some of the characters are singing can mix together with some of the sounds of a brand new day.

PETER ARNOTT
2023

Group Portrait in a Summer Landscape was first performed at the Pitlochry Festival Theatre on 25th August 2023, a Pitlochry Festival Theatre and Royal Lyceum Edinburgh co-production. The cast was as follows:

Rennie	John Michie
Moon	Benny Young
Edie	Deirdre Davis
Emma	Sally Reid
Kath	Patricia Panther
Frank	Keith Macpherson
Charlie	Matthew Trevannion
Jitka	Nalini Chetty
Will	Robbie Scott

Writer	Peter Arnott
Director	David Greig
Set & Costume Designer	Jessica Worrall
Lighting Designer	Simon Wilkinson
Composer & Sound Designer	Pippa Murphy
Fight Director	Robin Hellier
Assistant Director	Viv Groskop
Stage Manager	Katy Nicolson
Deputy Stage Manager (floor)	Chariya Glasse-Davies
Deputy Stage Manager (book)	Katie Marie Galbraith
Assistant Stage Manager	Rebecca Gorman

CAST

John Michie | Actor *(Rennie)*

John's first job in theatre was as a stage hand at the old Traverse Theatre in Edinburgh's Grassmarket. Thirty years later he returned to the Traverse to perform in *Grain in the Blood* and *The Mack* (an Tran Myr Production), both by Rob Drummond.

His last production at Edinburgh's Lyceum was as Leontes in *The Winter's Tale*. Most recently he played John Rebus in Ian Rankin's *A Game called Malice* at Hornchurch Theatre.

On TV he's probably best known as DI Robbie Ross in *Taggart* and more recently as Guy Self in *Holby City*, as well as a stint in *Coronation Street* as Karl Munro.

Most recent TV appearances: *Death in Paradise* and *London Kills*. Film work includes playing Tony Fitzjohn in *To Walk with Lions* with Richard Harris.

Nalini Chetty| Actor *(Jitka)*

Edinburgh born Nalini studied Drama at Bristol University before training at Bristol Old Vic Theatre School. She then lived all over the UK before returning to Scotland to perform in David Greig's acclaimed *Yellow Moon* and later to join the cast of BBC1 Scotland's *River City*. She has since worked extensively in TV, theatre and radio. Recent theatre credits include: *Standby* (STC); *Cyrano* (Citizens Theatre/NTS); *Ma; Pa and The Little Mouths* (Tron); *A Safe Place* and *The Archivist* (NTS/Oran Mor). TV and Film: *River City* (BBC1); *Karen Pirie* (ITV); *Crime 2* (Buccaneer/ITV); *Justice* (LA productions/BBC); *Taggart* (STV) and *Hula* (Braw Films). In 2023 she will appear in Gregory Burke's new ITV Drama *Six-Four* as DS Shereen Rahman. Radio: *Puellae; A World Elsewhere; Angel of Market Street* and *The Return* (all BBC R4) and *Venice Preserved* (BBC R3).

As a writer Nalini has written regularly for the BBC, CBeebies and C4. Original credits include: *Puellae* and *The Infinity Pool* (both BBC R4); *Finding Noor* (Ankur/Citizens) and *Kontomble; The Shaman and The Boy* (Oran Mor/NTS/ Traverse). She also presents BBC Scotland podcast *The Reveal* which can be found on BBC sounds.

Nalini is delighted to be part of the Pitlochry company this year and would like to thank her husband Alan for 'holding the fort' with her 'wee yins' Luca and Mara-Kate.

Deirdre Davis | Actor *(Edie)*

Deirdre graduated from the Royal Scottish Academy of Music and Drama in 1991. She has worked for many theatre companies, including the Tron Theatre, Perth Rep and 7:84 Theatre. Deirdre first worked at Pitlochry in 1999, when she appeared in *The Summertime Is Come* with Jimmy Logan and Edith McArthur. Since then, she's returned to Pitlochry several times, appearing in *The Magistrate, Heartbreak House, Cinderella, Sleeping Beauty* and *Monarch of The Glen, Blithe Spirit, Heritage, North and South*, and she was also a part of Pitlochry Festival Theatre's Winter Ensemble 2021.

Deirdre has appeared in consecutive Pitlochry seasons, most recently in *Sherlock Holmes: A Study in Lipstick, Ketchup and Blood, Private Lives, Noises Off* and *Little Women* during the Summer 2022 season and Pitlochry Festival Theatre's 2022 Christmas production *Peter Pan and Wendy*. Outwith Pitlochry Festival Theatre, in recent years she has played Nora in Rona Munro's *Bold Girls* at the Citizens Theatre, Glasgow and spent 14 years playing Eileen Donachie in BBC Scotland's *River City*. Deirdre is delighted to return for Pitlochry Festival Theatre's Summer Season 2023.

Keith Macpherson | Actor *(Frank)*

Keith was born in Edinburgh, and trained at RSAMD and L'École Jacques Lecoq. He is delighted to return to Pitlochry after performing in the 2022 season, in S*unshine on Leith, Noises Off* and *Under Another Sky*. Other stage credits include: *Il Trittico* (Scottish Opera); *The Yellow Door* (Lyceum/EIBF); *Selkie* (A Play, A Pie and A Pint); R*apunzel, Bauble Trouble, Museum of Dreams, Waiting for Godot, Desire Under the Elms, Peter Pan, The Wizard of Oz* (Citizens Theatre); Y*ellow Moon, The Monster in the Hall* (Citizens/NTS); *Light Boxes* (Gridiron); *Decky Does a Bronco (*Gridiron/Almeida); *James and the Giant Peach* (Dundee Rep); *The Yes/No Plays* (Traverse); *Horizontal Collaboration* (David Leddy/Fire Exit); *Henry V* (Bard in the Botanics); *Rogue Herries* (Theatre by the Lake); *Mother Courage, Clutter Keeps Company* (Birds of Paradise); *A Christmas Carol* (Cumbernauld Theatre); *Hamlet* (MYT Theatre); *This Time With Feeling, Timeless* (Suspect Culture); *Para Handy* (Warehouse Theatre); *Funny* (Reeling and Writhing); *4.48 Psychosis* (Sweetscar/ Cumbernauld Theatre/Tramway); F*aust, The Prime of Miss Jean Brodie, Arsenic and Old Lace* (Edinburgh Lyceum); *Trojan Women (*Theatre Cryptic); *Private Agenda, Factory Girls, the Trial* (7:84); *The Lost Child* (Chichester Festival Theatre); *Invisible Man* (Vanishing Point); *Brave* (Communicado);

The Canterbury Tales (Rejects' Revenge); *Making Room for Camille* (AwareHaus); *Rafferty's Café* (Quondam); *Little Victories, Sunset Song* (TAG); *Macbeth* (Chester Gateway); *Media Star* (Theatre Workshop); *Bloodknot, Piaf, Twelfth Night* (Brunton Theatre).

Audio/Radio includes: *Donald and Benoit* (Pitlochry Festival theatre); *The Chronycle* (BBC Radio Scotland). Film includes: *Stan and Ollie*. TV includes: *Taggart, Silent Witness.*

Patricia Panther | Actor *(Kath)*

Patricia Panther is an actress, composer and sound designer based in Glasgow. Acting credits include; *Peter Pan and Wendy* (Pitlochry Festival Theatre); *Annika* (Black Camel Pictures); *Orphans* (National Theatre of Scotland); *The Last Bus* (Hurricane Films, Head Gear Films); *Trust Me* (BBC One); *Glasgow Girls* (National Theatre of Scotland); *Scot Squad* (BBC One); *Logan High* (BBC One); *Lament to Sheku Bayoh* (National Theatre of Scotland and Lyceum Theatre); *Dark Sense* (Encaptivate Films); *Arabian Nights* (Lyceum Theatre). Composer credits include; composition and sound design for *Ghost Light* (Edinburgh International Festival, National Theatre of Scotland and BBC Scotland); *Fibres* (Stellar Quines and Citizens Theatre); *Future Of Theatre* (Traverse Theatre); *Glasgow Girls* (National Theatre of Scotland and Raw Material); *The Last Queen Of Scotland* (Dundee Rep, Stellar Quines and National Theatre of Scotland); *Rites* (Contact Theatre and National Theatre of Scotland); *Once You See The Smoke* (Scottish Youth Theatre); *Sonic Séance* (Project X, Tramway and CCA).

Sally Reid | Actor *(Emma)*

Theatre includes: *Shirley Valentine* (Pitlochry Festival Theatre); *Sally* (Oran Mor); *Cinderfella, The Ugly One, Three Sisters* (Tron Theatre); *Wendy and Peter Pan, Union, Guid Sisters* (Royal Lyceum); *Rhinoceros* (Eif/Lyceum); *The James Plays* (Nts); *Great Expectations, Time and The Conways* (Dundee Rep); *Blithe Spirit* (Perth Horsecross); *Days of Wine and Roses* (nominated Best Actress Cats Awards 2013); *Doubt* (Theatre Jezebel); *Sunset Song* (HMT, Aberdeen); *The Wall* (nominated Best Actress Cats Awards 2008); *The Ducky, The Chooky Brae* (Borderline). TV includes: *Karen Pirie, Annika, Group, River City, Scot Squad, Only an Excuse, Two Doors Down*. Sally attended the School at Steppenwolf in Chicago where she trained in Meisner, Viewpoints and Improvisation with ensemble members.

Robbie Scott | Actor *(Will)*

Robbie is a young actor from the North East of Scotland and is a 2021 graduate from ArtsEd. Credits include Peter Pan in *Peter Pan and Wendy* (Pitlochry Festival Theatre) and Dick Whittington in *Dick Whittington* (Yvonne Arnaud Theatre, Guildford). Workshops include Renton in *Trainspotting*. Credits while training include Gus the Theatre Cat in *Cats* and Shalford in *Kipps*.

Matthew Trevannion | Actor *(Charlie)*

Matthew trained on the BA Acting Course at Rose Bruford College. Theatre includes: *War Horse* (National Theatre); *The Curious Incident of the Dog in the Nighttime* (Gielgud Theatre); *Fiji Land* (Southwark Playhouse); *Beautiful Burnout* (Frantic Assembly); *Othello* (Frantic Assembly); *Dr Dee* (ENO); *Little Dogs* (Frantic Assembly/National Theatre Wales); *Hamlet* (Young Vic); *Love Steals Us from Loneliness* (National Theatre Wales); *Bright Unconquered Sons* (Pleasance Theatre); Bent, *Journey's End* (Broadway Theatre); *Here's Tommy* (Kings Head Theatre); *Exit the King* (Tabard Theatre); *Divorce Me, Darling!* (Union Theatre); *Stig of the Dump* (Hereford Courtyard Theatre).

TV includes: *Kaos* (Netflix); *Wanderlust* (BBC/Netflix); *This World: The Bunker* (BBC). Radio includes: *English Rose, The Attendant* and *Wild Swimming* (BBC Radio 4).

Benny Young | Actor *(Moon)*

Recent theatre: *Don Quixote* (Perth Theatre); *A Christmas Carol* (Glasgow Citizens'); *Midsummer* (NTS); *Eulogy* (Glasgow Tran Myr/Edinburgh Traverse); *Hay Fever* (Citizens'/Lyceum); *Monarch of the Glen* (Pitlochry Festival Theatre); *Still Game Live* (Phil McIntyre); *The Tempest* (Xinchan Performing Arts); *Waiting for Godot* (Lyceum's 50th Anniversary); *Unfaithful* (Traverse, Winner of The Stage Award for Acting Excellence); *Macbeth* (MIF/Armory Park, New York); *Philadelphia, Here I Come!* (Donmar); *The Resistible Rise of Arturo Ui* (CFT / West End); and *27, A Christmas Carol, The Wheel, Be Near Me,* and *Six Characters in Search of an Author* (all NTS). Previously he has spent seasons with the National, the RSC and The Wrestling School. Recent television and film: *Shetland* (ITV); *Good Omens; Scot Squad; Still Game; One Day Like This; Garrow's Law; Waking the Dead; Spooks* (all BBC). Film credits include: Tom Harper's *Wild Rose* (Three Chords Production Ltd); David Mackenzie's *Outlaw King* (Sigma Films/Netflix); *Chariots of Fire* (Enigma Productions); *Out of Africa* (Mirage Entertainment/Universal Pictures); *Funny Man* (Encore Entertainment).

PRODUCTION

Peter Arnott | Writer

Born in Glasgow in 1962, Peter is the writer of some 50 professionally produced stage plays starting with *White Rose* and *The Boxer Benny Lynch* in 1985. These include the award winning *The Breathing House* (Lyceum 2003, TMA Best New Play 2003) and *Why Do You Stand There in the Rain?* (Pepperdine University, Edinburgh Fringe First 2012). His musical play *Janis Joplin: Full Tilt* toured extensively; his adaptation of *Monarch of the Glen* at Pitlochry Festival Theatre won the CATS Award for Best New Scottish Play of 2017/18; *The Signalman* won the CATS award for 2019/20. He has been Writer in Residence at the Tron and the Traverse as well as at The National Library of Scotland and with the Genomics Forum and IASH at Edinburgh University. His novel, *Moon Country*, was published by Vagabond Voices in 2015.

David Greig | Director

David is a multi award-winning playwright who became the Artistic Director of the Royal Lyceum Edinburgh in 2015. David's most notable plays include *The Events, The Strange Undoing of Prudencia Hart, Midsummer, Dunsinane* and *Europe*. More recently, David's new stage adaptation of *Solaris*, based on Stanislaw Lem's 1961 soviet science fiction novel, was co-produced by The Lyceum, Malthouse Theatre in Melbourne Australia and The Lyric Hammersmith.

In 2019, David teamed up with original creators Bill Forsyth and Mark Knopfler to adapt the international hit film *Local Hero* for the stage, which premiered in Edinburgh. David's new stage adaptation of Joe Simpson's best-selling 1988 memoir *Touching the Void*, which was co-produced by

The Lyceum and Bristol Old Vic, enjoyed a run at The Duke of York in London's West End in 2019/20. His other adaptations include Strindberg's *Creditors* (2018), Aeschylus' *The Suppliant Women* (2016) and *The Lorax* (2015). David wrote the book for *Charlie and the Chocolate Factory*, which opened in the West End in 2013 and then transferred to Broadway in 2017.

Pippa Murphy | Composer & Sound Designer

Pippa Murphy is an award-winning composer and sound designer who scores for film, theatre and dance. Pippa was classically trained on piano, violin and percussion from an early age and completed her BMus, MA and PhD in instrumental and sound composition at The University of Birmingham. She is currently Artist in Residence at the Royal Botanic Gardens.

Theatre credits: *Enough of Him* (NTS, Pitlochry Theatre); *Truth's a Dog* (Lyceum Theatre); *Orphans* (National Theatre of Scotland); A*n Edinburgh Christmas Carol* (Royal Lyceum Theatre, Edinburgh); *Total Immediate Collective Imminent Terrestrial Salvation* (Edinburgh International Festival/ Royal Court, National Theatre Scotland and Tim Crouch); *Lost at Sea (*Perth Horsecross); *Red Lion* (Rapture Theatre); *Wind Resistance* (Royal Lyceum Theatre); *Creditors* (Royal Lyceum Theatre); *Streetcar Named Desire* (Rapture Theatre); *Woman in Mind* (Dundee Rep); *Crude* (Grid Iron); *View from Castle Rock* (Stellar Quines/Edinburgh Book Festival); *Gilt* (7:84); *Strangers Babies* (Traverse Theatre); *Standing Wave: Delia Derbyshir*e (Tron Theatre Glasgow).

Film/dance/music credits: *Joseph Knight – Scenes for Survival* (BBC, National Theatre Scotland); *Aleister Crowley – Scenes for Survival* (BBC, National Theatre Scotland); *Message from the Skies* (Edinburgh Hogmanay 2020, 2019, 2018); *Anamchara – Songs of Friendship* (Scottish Opera, Commonwealth Games 2014); *POP-UP Duets* (Janis Claxton Dance, National Museums of Scotland); numerous arrangements (BBC Scottish Symphony Orchestra, Scottish Chamber Orchestra).

Simon Wilkinson | Lighting Designer

Simon works internationally as a lighting designer for theatre, dance, and opera. He has designed work for most of Scotland's leading theatre companies. Recent highlights include: the world premiere of Disney's *Bedknobs and Broomsticks* (UK and Ireland); *Islander* (New York/London/ Edinburgh); Vanishing Point's *Metamorphosis* (Scotland/Italy); Vox Motus's *Flight* (worldwide) and Robert Lepage's production of *The Magic Flute* (Quebec City).

Other recent work in Scotland includes: *A Mother's Song* (Macrobert Arts Centre); *A Love Beyond* (Traverse Theatre/Tron Theatre); *Peter Pan* (Pitlochry); *Undertow Overflow* (Scottish Tour); *Don Quixote* (Dundee Rep/ Perth Theatre); *Muster Station Leith* (Grid Iron/Edinburgh International Festival); the Runrig musical *The Stamping Ground* (Raw Material/Eden Court); *I Am Tiger* (Perth Theatre); *The Wonderful Story of Henry Sugar* (HM

Productions); *The Children* (Dundee Rep); *An Unexpected Hiccup* (Lung Ha); and *Christmas Tales* (Royal Lyceum).

Simon has won the Critics Award For Theatre in Scotland for Best Design three times - for *Flight* in 2018, *Black Beauty* in 2017 and *Bondagers* in 2015. Over the years, his lighting has created a Guinness World Record, brought 30,000 people to a windswept Highland Forest and caused reports of an alien invasion.

Jessica Worrall | Set & Costume Designer

Theatre Design work includes: *Red Riding Hood, Comedy of Errors* (Citizens Theatre); *Henry IV parts 1 and 2, Henry V, Two Noble Kinsmen* (Shakespeare's Globe); *After Edward, Edward II, The Treason Trial of Walter Raleigh, The Captive Queen*, (Sam Wanamaker Playhouse); *Educating Rita* (Dukes Theatre); *Rites* (National Theatre of Scotland); *Grit: The Martyn Bennett Story* (Tramway Glasgow); *When We Are Married, For Love or Money, We Are Three Sisters, They Don't Pay? We Won't Pay, She Stoops to Conquer, Love's Labours Lost, Wars of the Roses, Lisa's Sex Strike, School for Scandal, Macbeth, Oedipus, Crack'd Pot, King John, Twelfth Night, Antony and Cleopatra, Richard III and A Midsummer Night's Dream* (Northern Broadsides); *Alice through the Looking Glass* (the egg, Bath); *Huxleys Lab* (Grid Iron,Edinburgh); *The Last Straw, Ghost Sonata, The Obituary Show, A Song without Sound?* (People Show).

Film design: *The Last Day, The Jossers* (dir. Gareth Brierley/People Show); *Death of a Double Act* (dir. Christine Entwisle); *The Loss of Sexual Innocence* (dir. Mike Figgis).

Viv Groskop | Assistant Director

Viv is a playwright, comedian and author. Her plays include *One Summer in Luka* (BBC Radio 3) about the Ukrainian village where Chekhov wrote his first play *The Wood Demon* and *For Love Nor Money* (BBC Radio 4) about the Ukrainian refugee experience in the UK. She is the author of six books, including the best-sellers *The Anna Karenina Fix: Life Lessons from Russian Literature* and *How to Own the Room: Women and the Art of Brilliant Speaking*. She has taken five one-woman shows to the Edinburgh Fringe at The Stand and Underbelly. She is the host of the *How to Own the Room* podcast, which has two million downloads and is nominated for the British Podcast Awards 2023.

PITLOCHRY
FESTIVAL
THEATRE

Group Portrait in a Summer Landscape

Peter Arnott

CHARACTERS

RENNIE
an academic

EDIE
his wife

EMMA
their daughter

WILL
their son (deceased)

MOON
a family friend

FRANK
a former student of Rennie's

KATH
Frank's fiancée

CHARLIE
a former student of Rennie's

JITKA
Charlie's assistant

This text went to press before the end of rehearsals and so may differ slightly from the play as performed.

ACT ONE

George and Edie Rennie's beautiful house in Perthshire. A morning in summer 2014.

SCENE 1. KITCHEN

EDIE, wearing a dressing gown, is at the table drinking tea. WILL, a ghost, forever 19, is haunting her. No one can see him yet. EDIE goes to a dresser and looks for something. WILL watches her.

The sound of a car pulling up on gravel. EDIE continues her search. Car door opens then slams shut. We hear the car move off.

MOON enters with a suitcase and looks at EDIE.

MOON: Edie?

She turns, hearing the voice but not yet seeing him.

Edie!

EDIE: Did you remember the Tiramsu?

MOON: What?

EDIE: *(seeing him properly)* Jimmy! I thought you were the man from the delicatessen. They're in Dunkeld.

Pause.

He looks at her puzzled.

MOON: Have you gone mental or something? Because, if you have, I can always come back.

EDIE: You're awfully early, Jimmy. I haven't entirely collected myself yet.

MOON: I can see that.

WILL grins at him. MOON doesn't see him either. EDIE starts to absently search the kitchen again.

What are you looking for?

EDIE: Alka-Seltzer. Plink Plink Fizz. I know we've got some somewhere.

MOON: So, what's the matter with George, then? Is it true?

EDIE: What?

MOON: Independence!

EDIE: You know very well that Rennie likes it when people pay attention to him!

MOON: Does it have to be for <u>this</u>, though? Could it not have been something else?

EDIE: He's going to make an announcement next week.

MOON: How can he be so irresponsible?

EDIE: That's not really my area!

Pause.

Oh, I'm so glad he asked you this weekend!

They embrace, normality restored.

MOON: How's Emma?

EDIE: She drove up yesterday.

MOON: What's the matter with her now?

EDIE: Nothing! She's here for... the celebration. She's in London, selling art to the Russian mafia. I'm fine too, by the way, thank you for asking.

MOON: I did ask you!

EDIE: You asked me if I'd gone mental. It's not quite the same thing.

MOON: A delicatessen?

Pause.

In Dunkeld?

EDIE laughs, looking at him.

MOON: What are you laughing at?

EDIE: I'm remembering my playing Portia to your Brutus in 1962.

MOON: 1962? Oh my God!

EDIE: Our first year at the RSAMD.

MOON: *(waving away the reminder of age)* Anyone else coming today that I should know about?

EDIE: Banquo's ghost.

She crosses herself. WILL smiles.

"Fair Thoughts and Happy Hours attend thee."

MOON looks around. He looks at the ghost.

There are eight of us for dinner. I've ordered pudding.

MOON: Who?

EDIE: Colleagues. That's all I know.

MOON: God help us all!

EDIE: What's wrong now? You know what he's like! He doesn't tell me anything!

MOON: I'm thinking about the two of you being up here all the time... together. Rotting in the Celtic Twilight...

EDIE: Yes. What a lovely time we're going to have!

EDIE hugs him.

Get up the stairs to your usual room. I'll get dressed.

Suddenly he grabs her and they sing and dance together. Cole Porter's "Mountain Greenery."

They exit severally.

SCENE 2. CLIFF TOP

WILL watches as EMMA is with her father, GEORGE RENNIE. They are looking at a catalogue of paintings by Valentin Serov.

EMMA: The people Serov paints are ridiculous. But he loves them... That's the thing. Honestly, I've never seen such... affection... in portrait painting. Serov loves them because he's one of them... That Russian middle class... emerging like butterflies... just for a moment! Their absurdity is beautiful to him! They're so fragile, all of them... so tenuous... like he is, like the paintings are. History... war and revolution... is going to sweep all of Serov's people away!

RENNIE looks at her, then goes out towards the garden and the cliff top.

RENNIE: Why did you never get a proper degree?

EMMA: Dad, I'm organising a major exhibition!

RENNIE: Of a Russian painter I've never heard of!

EMMA: (*following and joining him*) That's the point, Dad... you've never heard of him! Even you don't know everything!

Pause.

I've never liked it up here.

RENNIE: In Perthshire?

EMMA: (*peering over*) No! On top of the cliff. Even when I was wee, I used to daydream what it would be like to fall off. You'd bounce wouldn't you? Off the face of it? You'd leave bits of yourself for the birds to peck at.

RENNIE: You never told me you were thinking about that.

EMMA: Yes, I did, but you weren't listening to me then either.

Pause.

RENNIE decides to share some information.

RENNIE: Charlie's coming today. He'll be here this afternoon.

EMMA: Oh, Dad... no...

RENNIE: With his new girlfriend. They're staying for dinner.

EMMA: Jesus! Why didn't you tell me that before?

RENNIE: I didn't want to upset you before I knew he could make it.

EMMA: Can I get upset now? Is that all right?

RENNIE: It's important to me that he's here today.

EMMA: Oh, it had better be important! It had better stop climate change!

RENNIE: Frank's coming too.

EMMA: Both of them? Coming here today? Dad... !

RENNIE: It's my celebration..!

EMMA: Mum's ordered food... how can more people...?

RENNIE: I originally told your mother we might expect Joe and Maureen. But I never actually asked them.

EMMA: You thought lying to Mum was a good idea as well?

RENNIE: I hadn't realised it would be such hard work. I had to speak to Joe and Maureen eventually... to make sure they knew they weren't really invited but to pretend to your mother that they <u>were</u> coming if she asked. It's all been very stressful.

EMMA: What on earth is the matter with you?

RENNIE: I don't need to explain myself!

EMMA: Yes, you do!

Pause.

Don't get upset.

RENNIE: Don't provoke me!

She looks at him.

Twenty years ago, you abandoned your final exams, on the verge of a first-class degree from Cambridge...

EMMA: Och, Dad...

RENNIE: ...and I was foolish enough to think that was the worst thing that could happen to one of my children.

Pause.

EMMA: I know.

RENNIE: You moved in with Charlie six months later! I still can't understand why you did that!

She doesn't reply.

You were always so careful. You always did things for a reason. So why did you do it?

She doesn't reply. He half talks to himself as she drifts back to her pictures.

It's up to you, of course, whether you decide to tell me! But it's going to be a busy day. I'd like to deal with things one at a time if that's all right?

SCENE 3. GARDEN

FRANK enters with a suitcase. KATH follows, very pregnant. It is her first visit here. FRANK looks at her expectantly.

KATH: So, he's definitely going to say Yes, and he's going to say it in public?

FRANK: Probably... I think so... maybe.

KATH: Och, Frank!

FRANK: Aye... well. He was an awkward bugger in the Labour Party for forty years. He's bound to be an awkward bugger now.

KATH: Do you think it would be okay if I sat down?

FRANK: Sorry. Of course.

They sit together on a garden bench.

You all right?

KATH: I'm a bit sick from the car.

They look at the landscape.

FRANK: Look at this place! The first time I came up here... I thought it was perfect. There were amazing people here all the time! Political, artistic people, not just the academics. There wasn't a book in the house that wasn't worth reading... and a lot of them were signed by the folk that wrote them! The pictures on the walls... the music... everything...

KATH: What happened?

FRANK: He changed. I don't know. He stopped asking people to stay... he stopped lecturing...

KATH: He stayed on at the University, though?

FRANK: Yes.

KATH: ...and you did all the work for him.

FRANK: Nothing's simple, is it?

KATH: Yes it is.

FRANK: In the long run, we're all dead.

KATH: No. In the long run we all go to heaven.

FRANK: How did I end up getting married to someone who'd say a thing like that?

KATH: You got lucky.

FRANK: You got pregnant.

KATH: I'm an innocent Christian girl. I didn't know what you were doing.

Pause.

FRANK sighs.

FRANK: You should have heard him twenty years ago. He made you feel like you could walk out of that lecture theatre and change the world.

He tails off.

Pause.

He sighs. She consoles him.

KATH: We can still change our wee bit of it? Can't we?

He looks at her.

SCENE 4. STUDY

In the course of this scene, we see EMMA bringing in a painting to the house. It is wrapped in brown paper. RENNIE is fetching MOON a drink.

MOON: So when did you leave the Labour Party?

RENNIE: When Blair rolled the troops into Iraq. That was the end of the old song for me.

MOON: And now you've gone completely bonkers?

RENNIE: (*grins*) Cameron would never have agreed to a referendum if he'd thought it would be close! It's devolution the Tories are after! If they can remove the threat of independence - or relegate it to an eccentric, minority interest - then they can pull devolution's teeth! That's why this referendum is happening! Cameron is calling our bluff!

MOON: He's calling the SNP's bluff! That doesn't mean you have to take the bait!

RENNIE: But it's devlotion I'm defending! You haven't been here, Jimmy, so you don't know the mess the Labour Party's making of this! It's awful, it's humiliating! They can't make anything even resembling a positive case for the Union! It's all threats! They're not even defending devolution! They're failing in their duty of hope!

MOON: Are you actually enjoying this?

RENNIE: Yes, I am! I'm enjoying the fight! I'm enjoying the democratic moment!

MOON: And because you're enjoying yourself... you're surrendering in public to the idiotic notion that the working class can solve real problems by hanging up some tartan curtains and not looking out of the window?

RENNIE: Jimmy, if you are looking to the British state as a vehicle for the expression of outward-looking international solidarity, then you are the one who's waving the wrong flag! I've got no illusions about Scotland, but the way our former comrades are falling into line with the Tories... on THIS question, like on everything else... is so degrading! It's embarrassing. It's enraging. Do you understand what I'm telling you or has the sun in Hollywood baked your brains?

MOON: Don't you dare dismiss me like that, George! You didn't bring me here for this nonsense!

RENNIE: You're here for Edie, Jimmy. You're her friend.

MOON: You're the one who's been married to her for forty years, George.

RENNIE: But she still talks to you. She doesn't hear me anymore.

MOON: *(impatiently)* Oh, for God's sake! Is this you feeling sorry for yourself as well?

RENNIE: What does that mean?

MOON: There is nowhere left on earth where self pity isn't in charge!

Pause.

You haven't actually JOINED the Nats, have you? Because that really would be despair.

RENNIE: I'm not quite in despair yet. I've still got you.

He raises his glass to his old friend.

Here's to the memory of the British Road to Socialism!

MOON: *(putting his glass down without drinking)* Speak for yourself, George. I mean that.

He stands and goes. RENNIE is frustrated. This isn't going at all well. EMMA unwraps the picture. She looks at it and then joins her mother in the kitchen.

SCENE 5. KITCHEN

EMMA enters as EDIE is preparing food in the kitchen. She is carrying the painting. We hear the sound of KATH throwing up. WILL is invisibly present.

EDIE: That's Kath. Frank's new wife. She's chucking up.

EMMA: You didn't make her one of your herbal remedies, did you?

EDIE: I might have.

EMMA: *(sniffs at a pot on the stove)* Lord, that is vile! Anyway, they're not married yet!

EDIE: Any day now! They seem very excited about it!

EMMA: Is she tremendously pregnant?

EDIE: *(indicates the picture that EMMA is carrying)* What's this?

EMMA: A present for the house.

EDIE: Let me see...

EMMA: I had thought of giving it to Dad for his retirement or his birthday. But I don't think he deserves it. It's a cartoon by Serov, the artist I'm working on. It's a sketch for a group portrait.

EDIE: (*she is thoughtful, uncertain*) A family and a house?

EMMA: It's from early in his career. He and his family were part of a sort of artists' commune in the country! That's his father. And that's Serov. Do you like it?

EDIE: Thank you, Emma!

Kisses her.

EDIE now carries the picture, testing different locations.

EMMA: What's Dad been saying to you about tonight?

EDIE: (*still looking at the picture, walking with it*) His great occasion? I'm just doing the catering. He's upstairs now, arguing with Jimmy about the referendum. The two of them used to shout at each other all night back in the sixties... only in those days, Jimmy was a Leninist and your father was a Trotskyist.

EMMA: (*following, as EDIE tries out various temporary locations*) Uncle Jimmy's back on television again. And in America as well... HBO! He's got a series!

EDIE: Has he really?

EMMA: (*teasing*) Have you still not got a telly up here?

EDIE: It was one of your father's attempts to control the universe originally. We came up here every summer with no TV so Will would eventually read a book.

EMMA: Never worked though, did it... ?

EDIE: Your brother hated to disappoint your father...

EMMA: He didn't hate it quite enough to crack open Catcher in the Rye. Or even The Hobbit... God save us! He'd end up crying, Dad would storm off to re-read Orwell's diaries... and you'd give Will back his Spiderman Comics.

EDIE: Some of those comics were quite good! He used to read them to me... or he'd read Peter Parker and Spiderman and I'd get to play everybody else!

EMMA: (*joining her to look at the painting*) You thought Will was going to be an actor like you and Uncle Jimmy.

(*quizzical*) Why did you give it up, just like that? Uncle Jimmy says you were good!

EDIE turns from the picture, on the brink of getting tearful. EMMA sees that. KATH appears in the doorway.

Och, Mum, I'm sorry... is the picture a bad idea ? I just thought...

EDIE: This boy here... looks like Will.

EMMA: Like Will? Does he? Do you think so?

EDIE: Isn't that why you chose it?

EMMA: No. Mum... I didn't... I'm sorry...

They see KATH.

Pause.

KATH: Hi.

EMMA: (*recovering*) I didn't see you there, sorry.

EDIE: (*introduces them*) Emma... this is Katherine... Katherine? This is Emma.

KATH: I didn't mean to eavesdrop... sorry.

EDIE: You're in our house, dear. It's bound to happen. But accidently coming across our grief is something we usually try to arrange after you've had the rest of the tour.

ACT TWO

INTERLUDE 1: Inside WILL's head

The Garden in the Past. May 1994.

WILL conjures the past. Recorded lines are spoken on tape by younger versions of the 'present day' characters. The following are heard only. They may be repeated.

YOUNG EMMA: *(voice only)* Will. Make yourself useful.

WILL: Why didn't you go to the Seychelles?

YOUNG EMMA: *(voice only)* I'm not seeing Hugo anymore! Keep rubbing before I freeze to death and the midges come out.

YOUNG CHARLIE: *(voice only)* You never told me THAT was gonna be here.

YOUNG FRANK: *(voice only)* That... is his daughter! She goes to Cambridge!

RENNIE: *(voice only)* Are you enjoying the view, Charlie?

YOUNG CHARLIE: *(voice only)* Are you trying to disconcert me?

RENNIE: *(voice only)* So, what do you think, Frank? Will it be Gordon Brown that Charlie is working for in Communication? Or will it be Tony Blair... like Charlie thinks it should be?

As part of WILL's reverie, RENNIE, in his pomp, is speaking to a TV audience. His speech is 'live'.

RENNIE: *(on TV)* Accidents... like John Smith dying... show us the choices we've <u>already</u> made. It's not just the things important people like Tony Blair want to happen! History is like the glaciers retreating, carving the Scottish and Irish glens! Dropping the stones they've been carrying... they are the accidents history leaves there for us to find and look at. Like the Scottish Assembly! That can't be stopped now, no matter how much important people want to stop it! There's nothing Tony Blair can do to stop that, any more than there's anything Gordon Brown can do to stop Tony Blair.

YOUNG CHARLIE: *(voice only)* My father killed himself when I was nine, professor. My mother raised us on benefits and a hooky job in Pontypridd Markets. I don't see anything wrong with security.

RENNIE: *(on TV)* Oh, there's nothing WRONG with security. But we should remember, in this country, that it's always security for Surrey we're talking about. Not for Pontypridd or Polmont. Are we ready to commit crimes for Surrey? That's what we need to ask ourselves! Because keeping Surrey Just The Same is why there's going to be a Scottish Assembly. Keeping Surrey Just The Same is why Tony Blair going to be the next Prime Minister. Is winning really the only thing that matters? Is everything in the garden only Darwinian? Does everything have to be the way it is?

CHARLIE: *(voice only)* I'm going to find your big sister, do you hear me? I'm going to find your la-de-da Cambridge-educated big sister... and then I'm going to fuck her...

WILL holds his head and winces. EDIE joins him, like a ghost herself in 'his world' in 1994. WILL also speaks 'live'.

EDIE: There are those of us who life is destined to disappoint. It's an animal thing.

WILL: What about me?

EDIE: You're beautiful. You're not like the rest of us.

WILL: Mum...!

EDIE: Just let me look at you every so often.

She touches his face and leaves him. He calls after her.

WILL: I've got a bit of a headache, Mum. Have we got any of those Alka-Seltzer powders? You know? Plink plink fizz!

WILL is suddenly struck with head pain. He sinks into the seat. He recovers.

JIMMY MOON enters, (in 1994) very hungover. He is ghostlike, unreal...

WILL: You slept late, Uncle Jimmy.

MOON: Give me your report!

WILL: Emma never sat her finals. The letter from her college went to the Glasgow house and she burned it.

MOON: Dear me.

WILL: Dad is thinking about retiring early and writing more poetry...

MOON: He's always thinking about that! Isn't there something you haven't decided whether you should tell them or not?

WILL: Is it that obvious?

MOON: It is to me! Was he older than you? Was he nice?

WILL: (*shrugs*) He was all right.

MOON: And you're all right?

WILL: Yes.

MOON: You can always talk to me, you know? Even when no one else is listening.

MOON kisses WILL on the forehead. He exits.

WILL's head hurts him for a while. Badly. He recovers. He goes into the house. His headache leaves some space for the present (2014) to return.

SCENE 1. KITCHEN

Back in 2014, stormy weather outside. The company sits and stands, eating an informal lunch.

EMMA: (*mischievous*) So who else is coming today, Dad? If Joe and Maureen can't make it anymore?

RENNIE: (*glares at EMMA, glances at EDIE*) Charlie. Charlie Gilligan.

EDIE: Charlie? Is this what you've been planning all along? Is that why you didn't tell me who was coming?

She looks at EMMA, who grins.

You told Emma?

RENNIE: Just for today, we're talking about my life!

EDIE: We're always talking about your life!

RENNIE: Charlie's bringing his new girlfriend.

EDIE: And when were you thinking of telling me?

RENNIE: Like I've already said to Emma, I wasn't sure he could make it!

KATH feels compelled to fill the silence.

KATH: I didn't even know he'd been a student of yours till Frank told me. Let alone your son in law!

EDIE: Nasty wee man! He always was! No matter how popular he is now!

RENNIE: Might Charlie's popularity not mean he's onto something?

KATH: There's always a market for cynicism. It's the easiest way to sound clever.

EDIE: None of you could see him for what he was.

EMMA: And what was that, Mum?

EMMA: Even then he was a vulgar wee thug. And a thief!

EMMA: A thug... and a thief?

EDIE: He stole ten years of your life from you!

Pause.

EMMA: That's not what happened.

EDIE: He was unfaithful to you the whole time.

EMMA: As it turned out.

EDIE: He never once got a proper job... actually teaching. He just went on television where you can get away with any old bollocks.

FRANK: Channel Four think he's a genius.

EDIE: Don't get me started on those people!

MOON: I saw him on the side of a bus in London. His face! It scared me out of a year's growth...

RENNIE: I tried with Charlie. I really did. And he laughed at me. He was just a boy... and I was his professor. And he laughed at me. I thought that took tremendous...

EDIE: Bloody cheek...

RENNIE: Instinct. He instinctively knew... that I wasn't who he needed. There he was, twenty two years old... my most promising student for years... and he didn't need me.

KATH: He's very good at what he does. But it's all... anxiety. He just makes you feel anxious till the adverts come on to make you feel better.

EDIE: Yes!

MOON: Is it wrong to be anxious now the world is burning?

KATH: We have to hope as well... People need to know they have hope. That's what I try to do at school, anyway. Offer the children agency... something they can <u>do</u>.

RENNIE: How do you teach them hope?

KATH: You need to trust.

EMMA: Trust?

KATH: That there's something bigger, behind everything, there's a meaning.

RENNIE: Oh. Are we talking about God?

KATH: Well, I am anyway...

EDIE: Alleluia. We're all doomed! (*brightly*) Shall we clear up?

EMMA: Let me do it, Mum.

FRANK: Let me help you...

EDIE: Shall the rest of us go out to the garden?

RENNIE: I've got a speech to write for next week. For Kath and Frank! About Scotland's future.

MOON: Best of British luck! May God guide your quill!

RENNIE: Thank you.

FRANK: Might I have a word with you, Rennie? After you've done the dishes?

RENNIE: Sure. If you want...

While the others exit, EMMA and FRANK load the dishwasher and wash dishes. They begin in silence. Then EMMA feels she has to speak.

EMMA: She seems very nice.

FRANK: Thank you.

EMMA: And she's a Nationalist?

FRANK: Yes, like me now. That's how we met.

EMMA: I don't know why you brought her here, Frank. You must have known what it would be like! No matter how hard she tries... Mum and Dad and Jimmy... will eat her with the celery sticks.

FRANK: I love her, Emma.

EMMA: That's nice. No, really... that is nice, Frank.

FRANK: It would never have worked between you and me... even if... if that's how... when you finally left Charlie for good... if you and I...

EMMA: I didn't leave Charlie for you.

FRANK: I'm perfectly well aware of that. I just didn't want to upset you.

EMMA: Did you bring Kath here to show her to me? You could have introduced us before now, you know? You might even have asked us both round for a wee dinner. Why didn't you do that? It's because you haven't told her about me and you. Have you? Your endless persistence... me and my moment of weakness when I said yes... just once... and your grand passion wearing away at me ever since? I'm still your secret, amn't I, Frank?

FRANK: You know who you sound like? When you talk like that? When you're cruel like that...?

EMMA: I was married to him for ten years. Some of his style was bound to rub off.

FRANK: Why is he coming here? Why did your Dad have to ask him?

EMMA: Because Dad's playing a game, Frank. He's playing one of his mind games with all of us.

FRANK: What kind of game?

EMMA: I don't know. Maybe you should get Kath to ask God about it...

FRANK exits, going into the house. EMMA stares ahead of her. The phone starts ringing.

INTERLUDE 2: STUDY 1994

WILL conjures the past again. Lighting change. He is with his father in his study looking at the books. RENNIE answers the phone.

RENNIE: Hello... David? Thanks for phoning back. Can I ask you to hang on a second?

(to Will) Sorry, Will... would you mind?

WILL: Sure, Dad.

WILL smiles and exits..but sneaks back to eavesdrop..

RENNIE: Emma! EMMA!

A moment. EMMA enters. We realise WILL is listening at the door.

YOUNG EMMA: What is it?

RENNIE: Sit. Listen.

She stays standing

RENNIE: *(on phone)* Sorry, Yes, yes. It's about Emma.

YOUNG EMMA: *(alarmed)* Dad!

RENNIE: *(laughs on phone)* Yes, it is a situation, isn't it? A situation with the boyfriend, maybe...

YOUNG EMMA: Dad... please don't do this.

RENNIE: I know, David. I wouldn't ask you for any special treatment. Yes, of course... yes... thank you, David. I'll speak to you on Thursday... Thank you.

He puts the phone down.

YOUNG EMMA: Oh, my God...

RENNIE: They'll let you do a viva. You need a doctor's note.

YOUNG EMMA: I am not ill... it's a lie...

RENNIE: We need to keep your options open... till you decide to tell me what this is all about.

YOUNG EMMA: I don't want my options open. I don't want to be examined anymore...

RENNIE: Is that really what's going on?

YOUNG EMMA: "A situation with the boyfriend?" If the only way you know how to help me is to make a bloody fool of me, then don't!

RENNIE: Emma!

EMMA: Leave me alone!

She exits.

SCENE 2. STUDY. 2014

The sound of rain. Lights change. RENNIE is at his desk in his study writing. FRANK knocks and enters.

RENNIE: Hello, Frank.

FRANK: Kath wanted me to confirm that you'll be speaking at Academics for Independence next week.

RENNIE: I'm working on my speech now.

FRANK: She also asked me... Do you think we might see a copy... in advance?

RENNIE: Of course! If you'll agree to flap your wings and fly...

FRANK gets to his real agenda.

FRANK: The department will ask you for your recommendation.

RENNIE: They already have.

FRANK: And do I have your support? Will you recommend me for your chair?

Pause.

RENNIE: No, I won't, Frank. I'm sorry.

FRANK: You're not sorry at all. You think you're doing the right thing.

RENNIE: I am doing the right thing. And my regret is quite real.

FRANK: I'm finding this very difficult.

RENNIE: Maybe I should never...

FRANK: Never have taken me on? Never got me to write my PhD?

RENNIE: Frank...

FRANK: I've been protecting you for years! I've been shielding you from the administration and the bullshit. Because I thought it was important... that you should be able to work...

RENNIE: Then neither one of us has achieved what we set out to do.

Pause.

He gets FRANK a drink.

I used to be able to think in public, Frank. That was my gift. I even made sense of things for you, once upon a time. It was a complicated world then, like it always was. But you embraced that difficulty, you wanted to bear the burden of it. And I loved you for that.

FRANK: But I couldn't cut the mustard, could I? We can't all be geniuses like you and Charlie Gilligan!

RENNIE: Frank, when I first saw your faces... you and Charlie, among all the other faces... I faces I wanted to teach. I saw courage... a refusal to retreat from complicated truth. But these last ten years... twenty years, if I am honest... I haven't seen those faces anymore. It's not that they aren't there. I'm just not looking for them...

FRANK: Is this what we're here for this weekend? For you to be honest? For us to be honest with you?

RENNIE: If you have achieved less in your career... than you might have done... it's my fault as much as yours. My recommendation now would not serve you now, Frank.

FRANK stares for a moment, laughs sardonically, getting angrier.

FRANK: Christ, you've got no idea! You have no idea how the world works! If you recommend me for the professorship...

RENNIE: I've told you, I can't do that...

FRANK: Listen to me for once! Listen to me!

He collects himself.

If you recommend me for the Professorship... even if you don't mean it... there will have to be an interview... and if there is an interview, they will not be able to get rid of me for at least another year, and I will have that year to find myself another fucking job. Do you understand now? If you don't recommend me for the professorship, I will lose my tenure! I will lose my fucking house. I am going to become somebody's father and I am about to lose my fucking house.

Pause.

RENNIE: I hadn't thought of it like that.

FRANK: Think about it now. You me that much!

RENNIE: All right.

FRANK: Thank you!

He moves to exit.

Your farewell lecture... by the way... your panegyric threnody on the theme of time... was the self-indulgence of an old man making poetry out of having nothing left to say.

ACT THREE

SCENE 1. CLIFF TOP

CHARLIE is on the cliff top. He balances at the edge of the stage, which is the edge of the cliff in the 'real world'.

KATHh enters and sits. CHARLIE wobbles then picks up a rock. He looks at it.

CHARLIE: Oh. Hello.

KATH: You're Charlie Gilligan...

CHARLIE: I think so. Who are you?

KATH: My name's Katherine McLean. I'm staying with the Rennies this weekend.

CHARLIE: You're the one gettin married to my old pal, Frank Galloway! Congratulations.

Holds up a stone.

This is a rock.

KATH: What kind of rock?

CHARLIE: I don't know. I've just made a whole TV series... about rocks... and I haven't got a clue what this is.

(calls) Jitka!

JITKA enters. CHARLIE holds out the rock

What the fuck is this?

JITKA: It's a quartz mixed with sandstone. Not at all interesting. *(indicates KATH)* Who is this?

CHARLIE: *(tossing the rock aside)* This is Katherine McLean... the bride to be of my dear, old friend... Frank Galloway. I've told you about Frank.

JITKA: (r*emembering, snorting with laughter*) Oh Jesus! (*to KATH*) Excuse me. (*to CHARLIE*) Is he here?

KATH: Yes.

JITKA: Oh, very good. This is very enjoyable. (*to KATH*) It is very nice to meet you. And look at you! You are huge.

KATH: Are you both here for Rennie's retirement dinner?

CHARLIE: Is that what the occasion is?

KATH: (*to JITKA*) I'm sorry... but where are you from?

JITKA: Brno. I was studying there for my doctorate in geology which was why Charlie hired me as a consultant when he arrived with his film crew... but my passion is for languages. So now I am a student again!

KATH: You're a student again?

CHARLIE: Aren't we all of us students? Is the earth not our perpetual university? But it does say Jitka's a student on her passport. Currently a student of the televisual arts... on attachment, aren't you, love?

JITKA: Yes... yes I am...

KATH: I see. (*to JITKA*) Well... perhaps you can tell me what it is I'm looking at?

JITKA: This is a glacial channel. There was ice here... for millions of years...

KATH: And these stones you're carrying... are these...?

JITKA: Xenomorphs. Yes. But they are much much older. Much older than the ice. They come from far away, erupted far to the north of here... then carried by the ice flow... see? The glacier carried them here very slowly... And when it went away, it left them behind for me to find...

CHARLIE: The retreat of the ice, by the way... in the last, rapid spate of global warming... was accompanied by a fortuitously concurrent genetic modification of wheat grass in the valleys of the Middle East... which opened up the possibility of agriculture. From which all societal development consequentially arose.

KATH: You don't say?

CHARLIE: Oh yeah, the entirety of civilisation is an opportunity arising from a change in the weather. And now that window is closing.

KATH: So it's the end of civilisation, is it? Or is that just television?

CHARLIE: No, I honestly think geology has a sense of humour. *(he turns to JITKA)* Still. Not to worry.

JITKA: No.

CHARLIE: We still have love!

JITKA: Yes, we do.

He kisses her passionately.

MOON enters

MOON: *(seeing them)* Oh, my God.

CHARLIE looks at him.

Hello, Charles!

CHARLIE: Jimmy Moon, you old fruit! How the fuck are ye?

MOON: *(dry as dust)* All the better for seeing you...

JITKA: Jimmy Moon? You are Jimmy Moon? The actor!

(to CHARLIE) Charlie... you didn't say!

CHARLIE: I didn't know.

JITKA: Mister Moon, I have loved you from when I was a little girl, when they used to show you dubbed in the Czech language.

MOON: That's very sweet of you.

JITKA: I know your face but with another voice! That's so freaky! (*she laughs*)

MOON: Thank you.

CHARLIE: I wanted to show Jitka the local fossils before we came down to the house. Mission accomplished!

MOON: That's nice.

CHARLIE: Shall we go down now, ladies... our master is waiting for us... and Jitka is very excited to meet you all. Aren't you, love?

He offers his arm.

JITKA: Yes, Charlie.

MOON: I'll be down in a moment. I'm still assessing the geography.

JITKA takes CHARLIE's arm. They exit. MOON and KATHERINE watch them.

KATH: This whole place is haunted, isn't it? Ghosts are everywhere!

MOON: You're a Scottish nationalist, I'm told.

KATH: I'm in the SNP. I'm an activist.

MOON: Are you really?

KATH: Is that a problem for you? Aren't my identity politics complicated enough already? Is that what you're thinking?

MOON: Not at all

KATH: It turns out that my being part of reinventing this haunted, imperialist wee country is part of the answer for me... So I don't have a problem with it at all.

MOON: Yes. Well, I grew up gay, Catholic and Irish in Lanarkshire in the 1950s. And I can assure you that the phrase "We are the people" was never intended to include me.

KATH: Things can change. Countries can change.

MOON: How pregnant are you?

KATH: Seven months. Why?

MOON: And how's it going so far?

KATH: I'm fine. Thank you.

MOON: What about Frank? I suppose incipient fatherhood must... change your life too.

KATH: It's more and more difficult for Frank.

MOON: At the University?

KATH: They're making redundancies.

MOON: Is there nowhere safe from The Hidden Hand?

KATH: Frank seems to think that it's here in this house... that freedom and peace and fulfilment... are right here.

MOON: And where do you think we can find these lovely things?

KATH: In the future. I think the desire for justice, to have any chance of meeting reality, roots itself in a community we invent, a community we can turn to meeting human needs.

MOON: And that's supposed to be Scotland, is it?

KATH: I'd very much welcome the chance to find out.

Pause.

Who's Will?

MOON: Pardon?

KATH: Will? I overheard... Edie and Emma were...

MOON: Will is the son... the boy who died.

KATH: Oh right...sorry.

MOON: That's why it's haunted here. It was a genetic disorder he inherited from Edie that killed him. Didn't you ever read Rennie's book?

KATH: No. I haven't got round to it.

MOON: That bloody book. It was such a success!

KATH: They all seem very... odd to me. Old fashioned. Emma does too.

MOON: Does she? I suppose Frank's told you all about her... She broke his heart... I think.

KATH: Did she?

MOON: But I'm sure he got over it!

She stares.

Perhaps I'd better shut up now!

SCENE 2. GARDEN

EMMA waits in the garden.

CHARLIE: (*calling from off-stage*) Rennie! Rennie! Where are you?

EMMA stands, bracing herself. CHARLIE calls again, still off stage.

I want you to meet someone.

CHARLIE and JITKA enter.

Emma! My God, but you're looking as lovely as ever. This is Jitka.

JITKA: Hello.

JITKA extends her hand. EMMA doesn't take it.

Pause as EMMA and JITKA size each other up.

CHARLIE: I bumped into Jimmy Moon at the cliffs there. He looked terrible. I thought he was doing all right for himself across the pond these days?

EMMA: He is. Can I get you a soft drink?

CHARLIE: Oh yes, please...

EMMA: Jitka? Will you give me a hand?

CHARLIE: (*to JITKA*) Go on, she'll not bite ye. I'll wait out here for you. Shame to make waste of the sunshine.

EMMA and JITKA go in.

SCENE 3. STUDY

EDIE enters to fetch RENNIE. He looks up.

EDIE: Everyone's here now. Charlie's in the garden.

RENNIE: I know. Thank you.

EDIE: How are you enjoying your day so far? How do you think it's going?

RENNIE: Everybody is very angry with me.

Pause.

I miss you.

Pause.

He holds up the book of Hardy's poems

I thought I might read this poem. I'm trying to learn it.

EDIE: Something of yours?

RENNIE: Lord, no! Thomas Hardy.

EDIE: You put the Glasgow house on the market? You did that already? Didn't you?

RENNIE: No time like the present. I didn't know if you'd be interested.

EDIE: Where were you thinking of living? I don't want you up here all the time.

RENNIE: Weren't we happy here once, you and me?

EDIE: Why did you bring everyone here, Rennie, for this... gathering? Whatever it is...

RENNIE: Perhaps I just wanted us all to talk to each other. Say all the things that have been left unsaid.

EDIE: Things are left unsaid in families for the very good reason that saying them out loud upsets everyone.

She moves close.

You play whatever game you want, Rennie. You enjoy yourself. I'll still be here tomorrow. When they've gone.

She exits. He follows.

SCENE 4. GARDEN

CHARLIE turns to where FRANK is hovering just off stage.

CHARLIE: I can see you lurking, Frank. Come out of the hydrangeas, will you?

FRANK enters

How the hell are ye?

FRANK: I'm all right, Charlie. You?

CHARLIE: I just met your fiancée. On the cliff. Did you not think you should go with her, her in that condition?

FRANK: I'm so glad that Emma left you.

CHARLIE: Now where did that come from? Is that any way to talk to an old friend?

FRANK: You're a savage. You always were a savage.

CHARLIE: Oh, so I was. So I am. And if you think my being here in this bourgeois fucking hell-hole is going to make me hesitate for one fucking second to put my fist through your fucking neck, then you are kidding yourself. Do we understand each other? Get in my face and I will fucking have you. I don't give a fuck.

EMMA and JITKA come back from the kitchen with a tray of lemonade.

EMMA: We brought lemonade for everyone. How are you boys getting along?

CHARLIE: I think our relationship is just about at par, thank you.

FRANK: Fine.

CHARLIE: Frank. This is Jitka. Jitka... (*he twinkles cruelly*) This is Frank.

JITKA dissolves in peals of laughter as KATH and MOON enter.

FRANK: What's so funny?

CHARLIE: Don't you know?

JITKA: Oh, Charlie, he is exactly like you said to me. Exactly.

KATH goes to the stricken FRANK.

KATH: Frank, what is it...?

CHARLIE: Oh, it's nothing, Katherine... merely the past becoming immanent in the present.

EDIE comes out.

CHARLIE: Mrs Rennie. You're a sight for sore eyes.

EDIE: Rennie's just coming down.

CHARLIE: And then the gang will all be here.

EDIE: That seems to be the idea. I've brought the champagne.

FRANK: Let me open that.

FRANK undoes the cork. Meanwhile RENNIE enters and embraces CHARLIE.

RENNIE: Charlie! Thank you for coming. And this is Jitka?

CHARLIE: She's heard all about you.

JITKA: My parents used to talk about you!

RENNIE: Did they really?

He kisses her hand.

JITKA: He is a real gentleman, Charlie. Not like you.

CHARLIE: No... not like me at all.

FRANK has finished undoing the champagne cork. CHARLIE takes the bottle and takes over actually opening it. He pops the cork.

What a marvellous gesture, Mrs Rennie. Are you sure we deserve it, now?

EDIE: *(taking the bottle, pouring out champagne into the glasses)* I'm sure we all deserve exactly what is coming to us.

CHARLIE: And isn't that the truth? Isn't that the inescapable truth?

As EDIE pours, MOON takes CHARLIE aside and speaks to him in confidence.

MOON: Charlie, I just wanted to tell you that you are one of the most relentlessly unpleasant cunts I have ever had the misfortune to come across.

CHARLIE: *(to MOON in the same confidence)*

And in your long career in showbiz, you must have met so many! I'm flattered!

EDIE has poured the champagne. CHARLIE leads the toast.

A toast. To Professor Rennie!

They all raise their glasses.

OMNES Professor Rennie!

BLACKOUT

INTERVAL

ACT FOUR

SCENE 1. FRONT ROOM. 2014

A big table. The end of a long, boozy dinner. Emma's painting is on a sideboard. WILL'S ghost waits on the company who all wear party crowns.

JITKA looks at Emma's picture of the family, and looking back to its subjects. RENNIE joins her. Everyone, except KATH, is rather drunk.

a) EDIE, MOON and EMMA

EDIE: (*indicating JITKA to EMMA*) What is she thinking, do you think? What does she think of all of us?

EMMA: They're talking about the painting, Mum. It turns out that Jitka knows all about it.

EDIE: Does it? That must annoy you!

(*points at RENNIE*) Your father is making a bloody fool of himself too... with your husband's bloody girlfriend. It's like we've turned into a Psychology textbook.

b) RENNIE and JITKA are looking at the painting

RENNIE: How do you know about him? I'd never heard of him, I'm afraid.

JITKA: There was a big exhibition in Prague when I was little. The Russians arranged it, imposing their culture on us! My father bought the catalogue, despite Serov being Russian! It was the most expensive thing in the house!

(*she indicates the picture*) The father here is Serov's father. But he looks like you. I even thought it was you for a moment.

RENNIE: I suppose it could be me. Who's the young man?

JITKA: Oh... that's Serov himself.

RENNIE looks closer.

He looks like your son. I read your book. Charlie gave it to me.

RENNIE: Did he? That book rather finished me off, I'm afraid. I didn't really know what to do next.

c) KATH and CHARLIE. FRANK watches. CHARLIE sees him watching

CHARLIE: It doesn't matter, ye know... what humanistic, feministic, multicultural shite you and Frank pump into the little bastards... Everything else in the world is telling them that a machete down your trouser leg is your only real friend... that greed, violence and terror rule the world...

KATH: That's just a lie and you know it! Television personalities need schools, and roads, and the NHS just like everybody else!

CHARLIE: Depends how well paid we are...

KATH: And teaching children social values helps them to live better lives.

CHARLIE: Better for who?

KATH: Better for themselves... for everyone...Democracy... society...

(*CHARLIE laughs*)

What is so funny about that?

CHARLIE: You're teaching them how to survive in a liberal universe, that's all! They just parrot that crap back at you so they can pass their exams! Your pupils would adjust themselves just as happily to the Hitler Youth...

KATH: You're showing of!. Like you do on the telly.

CHARLIE: Do you really think liberal "values" are going to be of any use to them as a survival kit in the world the way it's going to be in twenty, thirty years from now? When the planet burns every summer and floods every winter, do you really think it's going to make a blind bit of difference if you call yourselves the People's Republic of Bearsden and Milngavie?

(to FRANK) Frank!

FRANK: Hmn?

CHARLIE: What do you think? Your girlfriend thinks I'm secretly a liberal. I want to know what you think!

KATH turns to FRANK. But FRANK is drunk.

FRANK: Sorry, I wasn't listening. But the two of you carry on. You're doing very well.

d) JITKA, RENNIE

JITKA: My parents read your history of Europe. In Czechoslovakia in the bad old days... in the papers that got copied... What's the word?

RENNIE: Samizdat? My Cold War book? I'm honoured.

JITKA: But history is so dangerous, don't you think? History makes people crazy. Like in Yugoslavia, they all went crazy.

RENNIE: Yes, they did.

JITKA: The moment they were free to go crazy, they went crazy. Freedom and history made them crazy.

RENNIE: Yes. I suppose so...

JITKA: So what is so great about freedom and history?

RENNIE: I'm sure I can't tell you!

JITKA: But I thought you knew everything! My parents thought you knew everything.

FRANK: Once upon a time... you'd have tried to answer a question like that!

CHARLIE: Once upon a time, Frank, Jitka, in this world of lies and disappointment... your parents and the likes of Frank here thought that this man grappled with the very stuff of their lives and spoke to them from the midst of that honourable struggle. When he told them there was a shining path between the Scylla and Charybdis of Washington and Moscow... they believed him. But now he has reduced his vision to the pokey dimensions of an Independent Scotland. How the titans of the left have fallen from Olympus! Is it something like that, Rennie?

e) In the kitchen

EMMA and EDIE arrange glasses of Tiramisu on trays, while MOON tries not to get involved and to have another drink.

EMMA: When I used to see the two of you kissing and groping all the time when I was little, I found it quite distressing. Daddy was off teaching, and you two unemployed actors sat around all day... fondling each other.

MOON: We didn't have DVDs in those days.

EMMA: I can see what she gets out of you, Jimmy, but what on earth did you get out of her?

MOON: I'd no idea that one was required to calculate such things.

EMMA: You introduced Mum and Dad, didn't you?

EDIE: On Grosvenor Square in '68. Your father nearly got his head broken by a policeman on a horse. It was love at first sight.

EMMA: Married in '71, and I came along in '72?

EDIE: Yes...

EMMA: And you moved back to Glasgow in '75... when my Dad got a job at the university... when you were pregnant with Will... and you gave up being an actor? After about ten years in the business?

EDIE: Yes.

EMMA: Why? You were good at it. Wasn't she, Uncle Jimmy?

f) In the front room, the company has settled into a single conversation

CHARLIE: You used to talk about the wire, didn't you, professor... the two sides of the wire at Auschwitz... that was your image of how the world was...

RENNIE: From Primo Levi... The Drowned and the Saved... yes.

JITKA: I had relatives who died there.

RENNIE: I'm sorry...

JITKA: It was history... it was freedom and madness.

CHARLIE: Well, the selection at Auschwitz was trivial... compared to what the selection by sea level is going to be. When the crops drown... when the fields burn, when the sands inherit the earth the survivors will happily murder everyone else's children when they attempt to escape from the weather. Vietnam, Iraq, Afghanistan... Somalia, Sudan, Syria... all of recent history... were are all just rehearsals for the kind of ruthlessness we'll need to watch as the children drown in the English Channel... And there will be no more use for liberals, Kath. Unless all of you witty, tolerant, wonderful people get wise to yourselves... we're going have to chuck you on the funeral pyre along with the rest of them.

FRANK: Who's we, Charlie?

CHARLIE: The survivors. The strong and the rich. (*to all*) But we shouldn't worry about it... no... we shouldn't mind a bit!

KATH: Why shouldn't we worry? Are you going to save us?

CHARLIE: Oh, no! We're not going to save you! That's not what's going to happen! We shouldn't worry because the population of the world, at the time of Mozart, was less than one billion souls... and now there are ten times as many and not a Mozart in sight! Well... a hundred years from now, we'll be right back there...there will be a billion of us left... and will that fraction of humanity mourn the mountain of the dead for very long? I don't think so. They'll have a few bad memories... maybe even some bad dreams... but our genetically enhanced descendants... or mine, anyway... will not feel all that bad that they've been selected from ten billion useless mouths who burned up the entire stock of fossil fuel in two hundred years flat... and turned the planet into a greenhouse? Why should they regret our passing? When what has this culture of ours been... but a fit of temporary, profligate insanity? I am an optimist, ladies and gentlemen, when it comes to the future of the human race. But I don't think there's going to be any room in it for nice, liberal people like you. It's going to get very ugly before we get back to Mozart! Your well fed, tolerant, inclusive civilisation... is finished. You know it and I know it. The difference is that I say it out loud: "good riddance to the lot of you... you were a lot of lying bastards anyway."

KATH: Is that how you sell survivalism to the rich? You tell them they're the chosen people?

CHARLIE: Who have the chosen people ever been, if not the rich?

KATH: So, you and all the other frequent flyers, you're going to be the only ones to escape the consequences of all the frequent flying?

CHARLIE: Sure we are! Why not?

KATH: Because there's still such a thing as democracy. There's still such a thing as justice!

CHARLIE: So your lifeboat of justice and democracy is going to be an independent Scotland? (*he laughs*)

KATH: That's what we need it for!

CHARLIE: You people will never learn, will ye?

RENNIE: There was only only category of prisoner in Auschwitz, Charlie... whose solidarity did not disintegrate. Not the Jews, not the gypsies, not the gays, not the crooks and not the communists... though of course the crooks did best as individuals, but as a group the best survivors were

The Jehovah's Witnesses. The other prisoners, according to Primo Levi, used to stare at them in awe and horror. Natural selection, at the level of the group... favours religious belief, the more fanatical the better... I don't think I want to be on a lifeboat the Saudi Royal Family, Charlie. Whether or not you think you've hired Mozart, they will tear both of you to pieces long before you get on board. You're too clever for them, Charlie... what makes you think you're all that different from the rest of us?

EDIE and EMMA and JIMMY return with their trays of Tiramisu. They distribute them under the following with appropriate thank yous and no thank yous. After everyone has been served...

CHARLIE: (*to RENNIE*) So what is going to happen in Scotland on September 18th? Give me a prediction!

RENNIE: At the moment? I'd say it'll divide around sixty/forty.

CHARLIE: 60 Percent for Yes?

RENNIE: For No. Forty for Yes. Forty five would be better.

KATH: It would be better to win. It would be better to get 51%. (*challenges RENNIE*) Wouldn't it?

RENNIE: I think the best possible result when Yes loses in September... and it's going to lose... is that it doesn't lose too badly... that the possibility of a different future... is kept alive... That's all. That will have to do you for the moment, Katherine.

KATH: (*appalled*) Is that what you're going to say in your speech?

RENNIE: I am going to say that given we have been forced into the position where we have to say something, that I am saying "Yes."

KATH: But do you believe in an independent Scotland or not?

MOON: That's a very good question, Rennie.

RENNIE: I believe... that the British State is shaking itself to pieces. And that consequently, Scotland will require something like statehood in the future to hold the future together. But when independence comes eventually... I want it to come with the same sense of boring inevitability that brought us devolution in 1997... when everyone knew what was going to happen and even if they didn't like it, they had to make the best of it. I don't think that's what's going to happen this year any more than I thought devolution would happen in 1979. I don't think it will happen... in my lifetime.

KATH: In your lifetime?

RENNIE: Oh, it might happen in yours, Katherine! But I was your age in 1979. And it was another eighteen years till 1997.

KATH: (*to FRANK*) I thought you said he wasn't going to be ambiguous!

MOON: Thank God for that, George! You know, for a while you really had me worried!

RENNIE I'll still be voting "Yes," Jimmy... if I live that long...

CHARLIE (*to JITKA*) What do you think? You got rid of the Slovaks, didn't you?

JITKA: Do what you want. It has nothing to do with me.

CHARLIE: She is so gorgeous. I do so love her. C'mere, you...

He fondles her provocatively. He is making her uncomfortable. She pushes him away.

EDIE: You were once married to my daughter, weren't you?

EMMA: It's okay, Mum...

EDIE: (*to EMMA*) No. It is not okay...

EMMA: Mum... I don't care...

EDIE: What is wrong with you? It is not "okay" for him to behave like that!

CHARLIE: Don't be ungenerous, Missus R... I'm a man in love...

EDIE: You're in love with what you've always been in love with...

CHARLIE: I'm in love with <u>life</u>... a quality you and your family once enjoyed...

EDIE: This is still my house!

RENNIE: That's enough, Edie. Charlie and Jitka are our guests.

EDIE: (*to RENNIE, exploding*) You do realise we are real people?... We are real! We are not just an audience for you and your bloody opinions...

RENNIE: I appreciate that...

EDIE: No you don't. You don't appreciate anything! You never did!

RENNIE: And now I never will. (*he quotes Thomas Hardy*) "Why load men's minds with more to bear... That bear already ills to spare? From now alway till my last day...What I discern I will not say"

FRANK: Is that Thomas Hardy?

EDIE: (*furious*) Oh, stop it, Rennie, stop whatever it is you're doing.

RENNIE: (*smoothly*) I'm dying, Edie. I can't stop myself from doing that.

EDIE: Don't be such a prick, George, you're not dying! You're just old.

RENNIE: I have pancreatic cancer that has metastasised into my spine and my oesophagus. I'll be incapable of speech in about six weeks. In about ten, I won't be able to breathe. In twelve to sixteen weeks, with or without treatment, I'll die.

(*to KATH*) I'll organise a postal vote for the referendum, Kath. But it may not count. This time, unlike in 1979, the dead can't vote.

Pause.

(*to the gathering*) I have taken steps for ending my life with a measure of control. That's why I asked you all here today... to tell you all together. And for all of you to settle... any remaining business you may have with me. I'm sorry if that's a bit awkward for you. But there we are.

Pause.

EDIE: Did you know this? Did he tell you this?

EMMA: No. He didn't tell me anything either.

EDIE: You ridiculous, pompous man...

RENNIE: Yes, Edie?

EDIE: You have done some selfish things before. This is the very worst.

RENNIE: Is it really? Have I finally hurt your feelings after all these years?

EDIE exits.

EMMA: Dad. Follow her!

RENNIE: No.

Pause.

Would anyone else like another drink?

EMMA stares at him and exits after her mother.

MOON: George... what are we supposed to say?

RENNIE: To me? Nothing. You are here for her, Jimmy. I already told you that.

MOON: ...she's your wife...

RENNIE stands unsteadily. He picks up the picture.

RENNIE: I'll be upstairs... if any of you feel like having a chat. I have some medication in the study.

Taking the painting with him, RENNIE exits.

KATH: This is obscene! You people! Look at yourselves!

MOON exits following EDIE. KATH leaves upstairs. JITKA looks at FRANK.

JITKA: Jesus... will you go too?

FRANK exits.

Charlie...? I'm going for a smoke.

She exits.

CHARLIE is alone among the debris. He exits. WILL clears up the plates.

FUGUE

The House and Garden

The next scenes take place, in 'real time' simultaneously, in different parts of the house and garden. EDIE and EMMA, and then MOON, in the kitchen. KATH and FRANK are in the upstairs bedroom. CHARLIE and RENNIE are also upstairs, in the study, while JITKA is initially alone in the garden, later to be joined by EMMA.

a) Bedroom

FRANK enters. KATH is packing quickly.

KATH: He's...mad...

FRANK: He's not mad...

KATH: It is not normal behaviour to serve your corpse before finishing the coffee!

FRANK: What are you doing?

KATH: *(she shuts the case)* It's not long past midnight. We can be home in two hours.

FRANK: We've been drinking.

KATH: I don't drink, Frank... I'm pregnant!

FRANK: He's my friend...

KATH (*she looks at him now*) Is this what friends do to each other, Frank? (*She looks at him scornfully, shutting the suitcase.*)

b) Kitchen

MOON enters.

EMMA: Go to him, Mum. Talk, to him... please!

EDIE: No! You talk to him.

EMMA: He doesn't need to hear from me. He's got nothing to say to me. He needs to hear from you!

EDIE: What about what I need from him?

EMMA: He forgave you once, didn't he?

EDIE: He forgave me for what?

EMMA: A couple of weeks before my finals... I was all set to sit the exams... this spotty wee chap called Findlay came up for a pre-finals party at my college. He told me about his Dad... Sandy Stirling... being a drama producer at London Weekend in the early seventies. And that his Dad and my Mum... you... had had an affair. That it had split up his parents' marriage. Of course, I pretended I knew all about it... I was totally cool with it... That's what they teach you at Cambridge... to pretend in a relaxed kind of a way that you already know everything... so, Findlay buggered off disappointed... leaving me downing one Pimms after another thinking of my early childhood, you had been having an affair with this man... And I didn't know if Dad had known anything about it... or had gone along with it or what?

EDIE: And that's why you came home. That's why you didn't sit your finals?

EMMA: No... that was because Findlay said... you went to live with him. You moved in with Sandy Stiling. You actually left my Dad for another man. You abandoned me when I was still a baby before Will was even thought of. I came home to ask you about it. But then, that day, my brother died... and it seemed a bit trivial to bring up anything as minor as adultery.

EDIE: Is this your part in the wee play your father is directing for us?

EMMA: No, Mum... he doesn't know anything about it. He doesn't know that I know. That's how we do things in this family now... without my brother to tell everybody everything...

EDIE: (*She begins to arrange the puddings on trays*) Well, I'm sorry we didn't live up to your expectations of parenthood. But I really don't see what either of us can do about it now.

EMMA: You can talk to each other! Either if neither of you ever talks to me! For twenty years it's been you up here and him in Glasgow... crossing paths for the occasional dinner! Now he's going to be up here all the time! You can't go on hating each other...

EDIE: Oh, Emma, we can! Of course we can!

EMMA: When you left him. He took you back.

EDIE: Emma... You're my daughter. I love you. But, you don't understand anything...

EMMA: Is that what you want? You want me to leave?

EDIE: Am I not speaking English?

EMMA exits.

(*to MOON*) As for you... just keep your mouth shut for a minute if you possibly can.

c) Study

Music. Jazz. RENNIE is behind the desk in the study taking his medicine.

CHARLIE sits opposite him. RENNIE examines him.

RENNIE: So, tell me Charlie, what is "the good"?

CHARLIE: What is the good of what?

RENNIE: *(he indicates the music)* Is this "the good?" For example?

CHARLIE: It sounds like somebody torturing a cat.

RENNIE: It's the John Coltrane Quartet... in Paris in 1961. Extending what it is possible for human beings to be. I think this constitutes "the good." Human beings extending the possibility of what human beings can be.

CHARLIE: You can always turn it off.

RENNIE: But what do you think?

CHARLIE: I think you're off yer head! You invited us all up here... to tell us you were dying? Why would you do a thing like that?

RENNIE: To see what would happen.

CHARLIE: Nothing is going to happen. You are still going to die.

RENNIE: Tell me what you think, then. It can't hurt either one of us. What is the good? How do we live the best life?

CHARLIE: Is this an exam or something?

RENNIE: No, Charlie, it's the only question I have left.

d) Bedroom

FRANK: He asked me here for a reason. He's telling me something. I just don't know what it is.

KATH: All he's telling you is to go home!

FRANK: He's telling me something about myself...

KATH: You didn't come here for a lesson from teacher, Frank!

FRANK: What did I come here for, then?

KATH: You came here for her!

FRANK: Who?

KATH: Emma!

FRANK: Emma"? Is that what's bothering you? Emma?

KATH: Emma doesn't bother me! You bother me!

FRANK: I do?

KATH: You can't hide it from me anymore, Frank.

FRANK: (*blurts*) You were flirting with Charlie.

KATH: What you did say?

FRANK: Everybody does.

KATH: Is that what she did? Twenty years ago?

FRANK: Even Rennie flirts with him. He's talking to him now... Emma flirts with him. You too It's an animal thing!

KATH: And it breaks your heart... that it isn't you?

FRANK: The thing... my thing with Emma... was years ago. It was nothing... nothing really happened... I know that now...

KATH: But you've never stopped thinking about her!

FRANK: He's my teacher, Kath, he's dying. I can't just leave!

KATH: Have you ever stopped thinking about her? For a single day? Have you?

FRANK doesn't answer.

e) Garden

JITKA stands smoking in the gathering darkness. EMMA joins her.

EMMA: Can I get one of those, please?

JITKA gives her a cigarette and lights it for her. EMMA takes a long, luxurious drag. Breathes out.

Thanks.

They stand not speaking.

f) Study

RENNIE: If we accept the thesis that God and history are both dead, that there is no future, and humanity is purposeless and doomed to extinction, how do we live in the meantime? How do we live better? What books should we be reading? What politics should we practice? What is the good?

CHARLIE: What do you care? You'll be dead soon.

RENNIE: I discover that I do care.

CHARLIE: Good for you!

RENNIE: What does that mean, though, that I still care?

CHARLIE: Old habits die hard!

RENNIE: Not good enough.

CHARLIE: It will have to do you, won't it?

RENNIE: I live in the meaningless, centreless universe that you've been selling me on television. I can no longer live as if I mattered! Or as if I am never going to die. But I discover that it does still matter to me what the good might be.

CHARLIE: And this impinges on me how?

RENNIE: The good... against all the logic of everything we know, impinges on everyone. I want you to tell me why you think that is.

CHARLIE: I don't accept your premise. (*he shrugs*) Can I go now?

RENNIE Your father killed himself when you were a child.

Pause.

CHARLIE: Christ, Rennie! What do you want from me?

RENNIE: Is that why you're so angry? Is that why your anger is so important to you it gets in the way of everything else? Is anger why you ally yourself with the scum you do just because they think they're "strong?" Just because they're rich?

CHARLIE: You want to "save me!" Is that what this is? You want to be my teacher again?

RENNIE: Twenty years ago I let you down. I failed you.

CHARLIE: Your failure, your cancer, your bereavement... they are all your problem...

RENNIE: Pain is <u>our</u> problem, Charlie. Because we share it no matter how ridiculous it is. Pain and fear is what we share... we deal with it together. They are not just things to be exploited! You are more than your anger, Charlie... It is not the only thing about you that is real!

CHARLIE: Why do I want anything else? How can I use anything but what I am?

RENNIE: Don't wave your working class authenticity at me! I am not Channel Four.

CHARLIE: You're finished, Rennie. Whatever you once were, this culture of yours, this civilization... is coming to an end. And that is the good. Your dying out... is the good. Satisfied?

RENNIE: Tell me what you really feel!

CHARLIE: It doesn't matter what I really feel! There is nothing I can say on television that is going to cure cancer.

RENNIE: Did your Dad killing himself, did your growing up in poverty and fighting like hell to get yourself an education... free you from the moral burden of being white, male and middle class? You work in television, for God's sake!

He coughs painfully.

CHARLIE: Are you all right?

g) Bedroom

KATH: Why didn't you tell me? Why didn't you say "Kath... the funny thing is, there's going to be this woman there this weekend... Rennie's daughter... and, do you know, once upon a time... I had a real thing about her..." I might have been a bit upset, secretly... a bit worried... but you'd have told me. Can't you see how much worse it is that you didn't?

FRANK: I didn't know she'd be here.

KATH: But you were very happy that she was... and you could show me off to her!

FRANK: Who told you? That I was in love with Emma?

Pause.

KATH: You did, just then. Nobody had actually used that word until you just did.

h) Garden

JITKA: (*finishing her cigarette*) We were rich once. My family. We had a house in the hills like this as well as our house in Brno. We were so rich we could even pay people to hide us from the Germans. Our immediate family survived the war... My father grew up ashamed of that. Of our being rich enough to save ourselves when all of our neighbours were killed. That is why he became a communist. Of course, we weren't rich any more by then...

EMMA: My father's father was killed in the same war. My grandad sank with his ship in the North Atlantic. On the way to Russia. That's why my father became a communist. There are lots of reasons for everything.

JITKA: My father was a communist till he hated the communists. Because they lied to him.

EMMA: I can see that.

JITKA: And so they stopped him and my mother being teachers and made him work in the tin mines in Ostrava... my father was a miner and my mother was a school cleaner when I was born and then the revolution came and they became teachers again. But they are still poor, they still drink too much and my Dad still misses the tin mines. And now I'm here with rich people. Who have always been rich! Who drink too much and hate everything. Just like poor people!.

EMMA: It's a tangled web all right.

JITKA: I want you to explain it to me. Tell me about your house. And why you are all insane.

EMMA laughs.

i) Kitchen

EDIE: He's right, of course. Not to have told me anything. I'd have wheeled him into radiation treatment... chemo-therapy... all of it... he'd be hairless and vomiting if I had my way.

MOON: I'm glad I was here when he told you.

EDIE: It ruined us, Jimmy. It killed us. What happened to Will. It didn't kill "me". It didn't kill Rennie. But it killed "us". I can't bear to look at him. It's been years... since I even... thought of him kindly. Will had his eyes, you see. (*cracking again*) You must think I'm such a...

She recovers herself. Smiles.

Pause.

MOON A monster? Yes. You are. But I don't see Will in Rennie at all. I see him in you. Your...terrible...

He breaks off the thought.

Pause.

EDIE: My terrible what?

MOON: Beauty.

Pause.

Let me take you away from here. We can call a cab from Pitlochry, we can go... anywhere.

EDIE: Why is it me who has to leave? Why doesn't he just go to Switzerland and get on with it?

MOON: Emma asked me earlier on what it was I got out of you in exchange for your friendship. Well, you and George and the children are the nearest thing to a family I ever had. And I can't bear you like this. I can't.

EDIE: What if I want to stay here, Jimmy? What if I am exactly where I belong?

MOON: Edie. Whatever the deal you made with Rennie... you've got to let him go now.

EDIE: Rennie?

MOON: No. Not Rennie... He's still alive. You have to let go of the dead. You have to let go of Will.

She smashes a glass.

j) Bedroom

KATH: I'm giving you one last chance, okay? It's me and my life, now... or it's this life here. And if you choose this life... these people... instead of me... then that's it.

FRANK: Why? Why is that it? What makes you the centre of the world?

KATH: There is no centre, Frank! I'm not it... but it isn't here either... this white, well educated, patriarchal paradise is no longer the centre of the world. There is no centre anymore... there's just us... making the best of it... doing what we can to live together like decent human beings.

He can't face her.

It's not going to be easy for me on my own. I'll have to... re-arrange a lot of things. It will be a pain in the arse! But I won't tolerate you dragging all this crap around for the rest of our lives. Do you understand? I've got a baby, and I've got a country... I do not need all this as well... this nonsense... it means nothing to me.

FRANK: It means something to me. I don't know what it means.

KATH: Okay. Get in touch when you work it out.

She exits with a suitcase.

k) Study

RENNIE: Maybe the fear of death makes us crazy... but it also makes us build cathedrals! One of us painted the Sistine Chapel, Charlie! He did it for a God that was never there! And yet the Sistine Chapel is! There are things in the universe now that wouldn't be here if not for us.. and maybe that's the good.

CHARLIE: Rennie... all your talk, man! About good and evil and art... Where does it get you?

RENNIE: We have to seek the good in ourselves, Charlie. There is nowhere else to look! But it has to be there or there is no hope. We still need some version of hope for the future, even if it's only to help us stay decent in the present day. We have to honour ourselves... You have to do that! You, Charlie. Especially you.

CHARLIE: Why me? Why did you ask me to come and hear all this crap?

RENNIE: Because I recognise you. Because I am you. Because I lost my father before I was born. I grew up with nothing... but I grew up with hope...

CHARLIE: Different days, Rennie... different times... we're different people!

RENNIE: But we can't live as if we believed in nothing anymore! We have to live at least as if we believed in something...

He coughs painfully, almost spent.

CHARLIE: Do you want me to pray for you? Is that what it is? Do you want me to recover your Holy Standard from where it lies on the field of Flodden... and lead the onward charge of the Scottish Enlightenment...?

RENNIE: If you don't, Charlie... I want you to feel like shit... I want to put my dead man's curse on your bones...

CHARLIE: Why are you conferring this on me? I'm not your son!

RENNIE: Because you could be a considerable man! Like I used to be! That's what I saw in you, Charlie, twenty years ago. And you're still stuck with it.

CHARLIE grins, understanding something.

What?

CHARLIE: You have a daughter, Rennie. Not just dead and disappointing sons. And counting both you and me, Emma is the smartest, most decent human being I've ever known. Has it occurred to you, even once, that you could be passing your burden onto her?

CHARLIE leaves the study. He descends the stairs as RENNIE drinks from his medicine. CHARLIE goes and sits in the library as RENNIE puts on his coat and takes a torch from a desk drawer and tests it. He takes a last look at the picture he got from EMMA. Then picks up the telescope, taking it and the torch out with him.

1) Kitchen

EDIE: We made a deal, Jimmy. Rennie and I made a deal. I'd come back to him... we'd come back to Scotland and renovate this house and have another child...

MOON: Yes. I remember all that.

EDIE: And I wouldn't be an actor any more.

MOON: I never liked that part of the deal. It was a mistake...

EDIE: I was happy with it. I was, Jimmy! Will was how Rennie and I dedicated ourselves to each other... He was our promise to live in the world the best way we knew... and we did. We really did. This was the best life that anyone could possibly have had, better than anyone will ever have again, if Charlie's right. But then Will died... And I blamed Rennie for that, and I blamed Emma... and I blamed myself. I blamed the whole universe... for being so cruel as to take my boy away from me.

MOON: You should tell George that. You should tell Emma that. Then you should sell this bloody house, leave this bloody country and never come back!

ACT FIVE

INTERLUDE 3

One last time, WILL conjures the past but this time the scene of his own death.

The House 1994. Thunder. The sound of rain. The generations have split. EDIE, MOON and RENNIE are in the front room kitchen drinking brandy. WILL, EMMA, FRANK and CHARLIE are in a bedroom smoking a joint.

MOON: (*sniffs*) What are they smoking up there?

EDIE: Lebanese, I think... (*sniffs*) Be good for your arthritis.

RENNIE: Maybe I'll take up star gazing. The children got me that telescope for my last birthday. It's still in a box somewhere. It's time... for space...

Pause.

How's Will's headache?

EDIE: He's all right. They're all up there together...

RENNIE: What do you think of those two? Frank and Charlie.

EDIE: Do you really want to know?

RENNIE: I'm interested in what you think.

EDIE: They're just more of your boys! One's a wimp and the other one's a shit.

RENNIE: I think they're both quite promising. Jimmy?

MOON: I can't tell any of your protégés apart. They're never fanciable anyway.

RENNIE: Please, both of you... forget I asked.

EDIE: You've been sending your faithless poison dwarfs out into the world for thirty bloody years, Bloody Blair and bloody Brown. To name but two.

RENNIE: Oxford and Edinburgh. Not my fault.

EDIE: They're all your children, Rennie. They have all gone out into the world thinking there is no God and they're God's gift. They are all your sons! You teach it! Now you live with it!

Pause.

MOON: What's the secret?

EDIE: Oh, God... now he's off as well...

RENNIE: Of what?

MOON: Happiness.

RENNIE: (*indicates EDIE*) Arguing.

EDIE: (*to MOON*) What's up with you today, anyway? You've been moping around all day.

MOON: I've been offered a film. A real film. The leading role.

RENNIE: Is that not a good thing?

MOON: It's...the director...

RENNIE: Yes?

MOON: He was a fan of Fairy Tale Storytime. When he was eight.

EDIE: It was a very good show. Very sixties... Puppets and Unicorns.

MOON: He was eight.

EDIE: It was a kids' programme.

MOON: But now he's casting me in a film... a proper film made with real money... because of something he saw when he was eight! I'm terrified.

EDIE: Is it a good script?

MOON: It'll win prizes.

RENNIE: I'm sorry, this is actor talk, isn't it...?

EDIE: Can I read it?

MOON: *(taking scripts from a bag)* I brought two copies with me. We can read it together.

RENNIE: What am I supposed to do in the meantime?

EDIE: Go and write another book!

SCENE 1. STUDY. 1994

Thunder. EMMA, FRANK, WILL and CHARLIE sit on the floor in near darkness. CHARLIE takes a big drag on a joint.

YOUNG CHARLIE: This stuff's... great... did ye get it down South?

YOUNG EMMA: Amsterdam.

YOUNG CHARLIE: I tell you what, I can't wait.

YOUNG FRANK: For what?

YOUNG CHARLIE: The great fucking off... I never want to see this poxy country ever again.

YOUNG FRANK: What about the hills?

YOUNG CHARLIE: We've got hills in Wales! I'm not interested in them either! I want to be in London! I want to be on the Planet Cash!

(tossing the book aside) Where does he keep his secrets?

YOUNG FRANK: We shouldn't even be in here.

YOUNG EMMA: Look, Frank. This is very you, I think.

She gives him the notebook.

YOUNG FRANK: *(reading)* "The true Romantic... Finds himself in Hell... And that Hell is improved... By his being there."

WILL: (*he reads*) "The purpose of man's life... Is to sacrifice himself to God... Now there is no God, however... The sacrifice continues."

YOUNG CHARLIE: I bet he wrote that! Is there anything the old bastard doesn't do?

WILL suddenly clutches his head. He screams. He collapses. The others step back.

YOUNG CHARLIE: What the fuck?

YOUNG EMMA: Will! (*calling*) Mum! Mum! MUM...

WILL moans. EDIE arrives. Then RENNIE. Then MOON.

RENNIE: Will?

EDIE (*screams*) Get an ambulance! (*to WILL*) Will...

MOON dials the phone.

(*to WILL, terrified*) What is it? Will...

MOON: Ambulance. The Stone House. By Rannoch.

RENNIE: (*turning on EDIE*) Why are we out here? What are we doing all the way out here?

Frank. Help me.

He and FRANK start to lift WILL. EMMA screams. There is blood on WILL's face, leaking from his nose, mouth and eyes.

EMMA: He's bleeding! His face!

Blackout.

The sound of rain continues. Ambulance lights. The others clear as MOON speaks to WILL's ghost.

INTERLUDE 4: OUT OF TIME

MOON: No one knew then... what had caused the haemorrhage. No one knew what had killed you.

WILL: I know. It's all right.

MOON: I can just imagine you saying that. I can just hear you. I hope that man who picked you up in Bennett's knew what a privilege it was.

WILL: I'm not sure he did know. I'm not sure he was really very nice.

MOON: He was a means to an end.

WILL: Yes, he was. I'm not proud of that, to be honest.

MOON: It's getting dark finally. It was dark that night too.

WILL: That's the thing about it out here. It gets really dark.

MOON: Gives me the creeps. No noise... no lights. Nothing reassuring.

WILL: The dark was okay. I liked the dark.

MOON: I saw... country dark, like this... for the first time when I was about three or four. It's my earliest memory. Your dad could tell me exactly when it was. He'd know the date it was, too, probably. I've never asked him.

WILL: How would he know?

MOON: Because it was history.

He takes WILL's hand.

My brother, my mum and I were in England somewhere in the country... to this day I couldn't tell you where it was. My grandfather was staying there, recovering... the Union, some Church thing... we went to stay with him... out in the country for a treat. Grandpa woke me up, about ten at night... And he said, "This is history, boy...you'll never see anything like this again!" I mind his smell, his quietness. His arms were like steel... those hands had marked my father... I think I already knew that. He carried me outside... where my mother was already looking up at the sky, holding my baby sister.

My eyes were full of sleep... but my ears were full of this low, droning noise, like a recording of a thousand bees with the tape slowed down. And there they were, gathering... like robot birds, circling... more and more of them coming all the time, like a spiral. Like some mechanical migratory species. The sky was full of bombers, just visible... There was no moon that night either. I was frightened. Grampa tried to pick out the Lancasters and Wellingtons for me, but I'm sure he couldn't really make them out. He was just guessing. He went quiet, too, soon. The light was failing. After a time, we must just have been imagining this great black wheel buzzing in the sky. We couldn't see them fade... but we could hear the noise of them moving to the east. Vanishing. We stood there for a long time, as the world returned around us, the sound of water somewhere to our left, from the burn. Sheep, I think. Then we went inside.

WILL: It was in the war.

MOON: What I remember was the noise it made. But I already knew the word. Grandpa had already told me that word. History. And why it matters...

He smiles at WILL awkwardly.

WILL: I like your stories.

MOON tousles his hair. Kisses his cheek.

We return to 2014.

SCENE 2. GARDEN 2014

Darkness is gathering.

EMMA: I can remember my mother screaming. A really terrible thing, actually... to hear your own mother making a sound like that. Will was bleeding from the nose... mouth he was unconscious. My father was driving the car. He'd been drinking, but he knew the road, and he must have felt that it was his duty. So he was driving... and my mother was screaming. Hours later, after the ambulance from Pitlochry had taken us to Perth, I remember sitting beside them in a grey seat in a grey corridor, holding my mother's hand, not looking at her. Scared of their silence, of the floor I was staring at, seeing patterns in it that vanished like dreams. And I remember waking up and wondering how I could have slept. And what had happened to my Mum. Why wasn't she holding me anymore? What was going on? Why didn't she love me anymore... or my Dad? Because I knew as soon as I woke up that she didn't. My brother was gone and the three of us were just left... there was nothing left to inherit... just a house... books... pictures...

JITKA: Really? Are you really like that? All broken up like that?

EMMA: Maybe that's why I bought the picture... the Serov. Despite it costing an arm and a leg. Because it's a family, the father at the centre, like it used to be. Perhaps I miss that. Perhaps I'm a conservative. Perhaps that's why I fell in love with Charlie.

JITKA: I can see why you wouldn't want to tell your father.

EMMA: Dad is so tangled up in himself... trying to make sense of things in the past... that he has never listened to me no matter what I told him. Or Mum either since... So I've never told either of them anything, I've never been able to tell them... for example, that even before he died, how much I resented my wee brother. How on the day he died, I was resenting how unconditionally everybody to love him. And then he died that day... And I'm stuck there... we're all alone and we're all stuck... time doesn't move. The ice... doesn't move.

JITKA: But this is nonsense! You love paintings... you love them! You want people to share your passion. You do everything to share your enthusiasm!

EMMA: I still can't talk to my parents. Even when it's nearly too late...

JITKA: Is it too late now? Already? Why are you confessing this to me?

EMMA: I don't know you. It's easier for some reason. I've told my therapist!

Pause.

JITKA: Is it because both of us were once in love with Charlie?

EMMA: Aren't you in love with him anymore?

JITKA: I was hoping you could advise me how to tell him.

A car engine starts. We see headlights moving.

EMMA: I'd better go and find my mother. That's the kind of thing that daughters are supposed to do.

She exits to the house.

RENNIE crosses the stage, turning on the torch as he heads into the wild with his telescope. JITKA, still in the garden, sees him.

JITKA: Mr Rennie!

She follows RENNIE, turning on the light from her phone as she exits.

SCENE 3. HALLWAY

EMMA, returning from the garden, meets MOON, coming from the kitchen. Meanwhile FRANK is coming downstairs in a state of shock.

EMMA: (*to MOON*) Where's Mum?

MOON: She's gone upstairs to talk to your father.

EMMA: Thank God for that! Please leave them alone, Uncle Jimmy.

MOON: Don't you worry! I was planning on having another drink, actually.

EMMA: Someone just left. I'm not sure who it was.

FRANK: (*as he reaches the bottom of the stairs*) It was Kath.

MOON: Shouldn't you have gone with her?

FRANK: I don't belong with her.

MOON: You don't belong here either, dear.

FRANK: I know that.

EMMA: She's left you?

FRANK: I think that's what's just happened, yes.

EMMA: Are you all right?

FRANK: I don't know yet...

MOON: Then you're fine...

CHARLIE, coat on, enters from the front room

MOON: *(to CHARLIE)* Charlie! Are you leaving us, too? What a pity.

CHARLIE: *(ignoring him. To Emma)* Where's Jitka?

EMMA: She was outside in the garden a minute ago.

CHARLIE: Tell her I've gone back to the hotel, would ye?

FRANK: Why don't you tell her yourself?

CHARLIE: Frank... I told you in the garden...

FRANK: *(getting in his face)* Lost control of your women have you, Charlie?

CHARLIE pushes him away. FRANK pushes back. They struggle. CHARLIE extricates himself.

CHARLIE: What the hell has got into you?

FRANK leaps onto CHARLIE, attempting to attack him. CHARLIE defends himself, sending FRANK sprawling.

Behave yourself, will you?

FRANK: I'm not afraid of you anymore!

He attacks again. This time CHARLIE hits him. Hard. FRANK goes down. CHARLIE holds his hand.

CHARLIE: If I've fuckin' broken something...!

He makes to leave.

MOON: Won't you stay for coffee?

CHARLIE exits. EMMA sits FRANK up. His lip is cut.

FRANK: I think I bit my mouth.

EMMA: What on earth did you do that for?

FRANK: I've been wanting to do that for twenty years. But I was afraid he'd beat the shit out of me.

MOON: He did beat the shit out of you!

FRANK: I know! I didn't care!

(*he laughs*) Do you know... I accused him earlier... Your Dad... I made fun of him. I said "have you asked us all here to be honest with each other?"

(*He laughs. FRANK is exultant.*) Well, that's what I've done. I'm being honest. I hate Charlie. I hate your Dad a lot of the time. I hate my job. I hate books. I hate my life.

EMMA: Frank...

FRANK: I want it all gone. I want to pull out my teeth. I want to shed my skin. That's what I want.

Out of nowhere, somehow liberated, he laughs. EMMA and MOON laugh with him.

SCENE 4. LIMBO

EDIE walks slowly up the stairs as FRANK, MOON and EMMA start clearing up, loading the dishwasher etc. They improvise bursts of dialogue throughout this scene. Laughter. Their burdens all somehow lifted... or at least lighter.

WILL awaits EDIE in the study. The lighting is unearthly.

EDIE: Rennie? George? (*to herself*) Everybody says we've got things to sort out. Where have you got to, you wretched man?

WILL: (*close to her*) You're too late, Mum. He's already gone.

She whirls, hearing and then seeing him. Startled, she stares.

EDIE: (*eventually*) Will? Is that you?

WILL: Yes. Of course it is.

EDIE: I don't understand.

Pause.

You're still dead, are you?

WILL: Oh, yes...

EDIE: I came upstairs to look for your father.

WILL: That's right... He's gone out.

EDIE: In the dark?

WILL: That's where he belongs. His time is over.

EDIE: You don't sound like you.

WILL: I've been dead for ages. You've forgotten what I sounded like.

EDIE covers her face.

What are you doing?

EDIE: I'm closing my eyes.

WILL: All right.

She uncovers her eyes.

Hello.

EDIE: What is happening to my mind? You can't be real.

WILL: This is where you came to find me. Twenty years ago.

EDIE: I remember.

WILL: I'd had a headache all day. You told me that fresh air and an Alka-Seltzer powder would sort me out. Plink Plink Fizz.

Suddenly she sits on the floor.

EDIE: What's happening to me?

WILL: It can go... either way... from here...

EDIE: What do you mean? Am I all right?

WILL: Do you want to be all right...? Do you want to go back downstairs in a minute... where they're washing the dishes... and find out what everyone's laughing at... Or do you want to stay up here with me. Do you want them to come and find you in half an hour or so. Because you can't take me down there with you, Mum. You can stay with me or you can go to them.

Downstairs, FRANK and EMMA laugh again at something MOON says. MOON and EMMA are teaching FRANK the "Mountain Greenery" song. EDIE looks to where the laughter came from. She looks back at WILL.

What do you want, Mum?

SCENE 5. CLIFF TOP

Minimal light. RENNIE, thinking he's alone, recites a poem as he looks through the telescope.

RENNIE: (*to himself*) We're the first generation on earth... who are free to speak our minds... And in the face of our extinction... we find we have nothing to say.

JITKA: (*steps forward, guided by the light of her phone*) Who are you talking to in the dark, you stupid old man?

RENNIE: Jitka? (*He sees her. She approaches.*) I'm talking to God.

JITKA: I did not know you were religious.

RENNIE: I'm not.

JITKA: Then why are you talking to God?

RENNIE: I've got to talk to someone.

JITKA: You should be talking to your wife.

RENNIE: It's easier to talk to God.

JITKA: Does He ever answer you?

RENNIE: He never has.

JITKA: (*looks through the telescope*) I thought God was supposed to be dead?

RENNIE: I've tried to kill Him. I've tried and tried. I can't get Him out of my head. (*he taps his head*) Like a tumour.

JITKA: So now you're going to kill yourself to kill God?

RENNIE: It seems to be the only way. But in a strictly Darwinian sense, we do seem to do better with Him than we do without Him... That's what I was going to write a book about... that's what I had to say... twenty years ago when my son...

JITKA: When he died?

RENNIE: Maybe it's only because he died so young that he seems so perfect to me now. Like someone in a picture.

JITKA: You came out here to talk to God about all this?

RENNIE: Do you ever look at the stars? My children bought me this telescope. But I never learned the maps. You have to learn the maps.

JITKA: (*looking through the telescope again*) Do you like the stars?

RENNIE: Why not?

JITKA: (*still looking*) Do you know about the gold girl?

RENNIE: No.

JITKA: And the bears?

RENNIE: Three bears?

JITKA: Yes...three bears, three beds, three chairs...three plates of...what is the word in English? (*she looks at him*)

RENNIE: Porridge...Goldilocks...

JITKA: ...what did you call her?

RENNIE: Goldilocks...the golden haired girl...

JITKA: Okay. Goldilocks. That's where we are. That's where we live...

She looks through the telescope again.

RENNIE: In the bears' house in the woods...?

JITKA: Where everything is just right. Just the right kind of star in just the right place in the sky... just the right amount of planets in just the right places... Just the right amount of metal for a magnetic core... the right amount of water in a comet that came at just the right time... and then dinosaurs getting hit by an asteroid to make room for us...

RENNIE: Yes. I know

She looks back at him.

JITKA: You "know!" Why isn't that chain of coincidences God? All those plants and animals and bugs... and then suddenly us... Isn't that even more amazing than God?

RENNIE: I don't believe in miracles!

JITKA: But I'm a miracle! Statistically! Don't you believe in me? (*She kneels by him*) You didn't know about me when you asked Charlie to come for your celebration. But I came anyway. To save you! Whether you wanted me to or not!

RENNIE: You've got one of those faces.

JITKA: What faces?

RENNIE: A good, brave face. I used to live... to see faces like that...

Pause.

JITKA: I will write a book one day. I'll write it in your memory. I will write a book about God. You must give me your blessing.

RENNIE: My blessing?

JITKA: Yes.

She closes her eyes and leans her face toward him. He touches her forehead with his fingertips.

RENNIE: There. Whatever it's worth.

She opens her eyes.

JITKA: It doesn't matter what it's worth. I have it now.

The sun starts to rise. They turn to the growing light.

RENNIE: If you look to the East from here you can see where the first people who ever lived here came from... There's a cup and ring that they scraped into a stone... where they greeted the daily miracle of it... another day... and not dead yet.

Pause.

JITKA: I've never seen a Scottish sunrise...

RENNIE: I wonder how they felt when they got here. I'm curious about that. I'm very curious.

They watch the sun rise, huge, overwhelming the projected stars. The cast has now all joined them.

BLACKOUT

END

ALSO AVAILABLE FROM SALAMANDER STREET

All Salamander Street plays can be bought in bulk at a discount for performance or study. Contact info@salamanderstreet.com to enquire about performance liscenses.

Peter Arnott Two Plays:
Tay Bridge & The Signalman
Paperback ISBN: 9781913630003

eBook ISBN: 9781913630034

Peter Arnott's brilliant vignettes about a 1879 railway bridge disaster imagine the lives and hopes of passengers stalked by death. The Signalman won Best New Play at The Critics' Awards for Theatre in Scotland, 2020

Chatsky and Miser, Miser! by Anthony Burgess
Paperback ISBN: 9781914228889

eBook ISBN: 9781914228308

Anthony Burgess expertly tackles the major monuments of French and Russian theatre: *The Miser* by Molière and *Chatsky* by Alexander Griboyedov. Burgess's recently discovered verse and prose plays are published for the first time in this volume.

Placeholder by Catherine Bisset
ISBN: 9781914228919

eBook ISBN: 9781914228940

Profoundly thought-provoking, this solo play about the historical actor-singer of colour known as 'Minette' offers an exploration of the complex racial and social dynamics of what would become the first independent nation in the Caribbean.

Outlier by Malaika Kegode
ISBN: 9781914228339

Genre-defying and emotional, *Outlier* explores the impact of isolation, addiction and friendship on young people.